Christmas at AMERICA'S LANDMARK Houses

2nd Edition

Patricia Hart McMillan
& David Strahan

SCHIFFER PUBLISHING

4880 Lower Valley Road • Atglen, PA 19310

FOREWORD BY
Christopher Radko

Designed by Danielle Farmer
Cover design by Danielle farmer

Cover photo by Gino De Grandis

Type set in P22 Zaner/Garamond/Minion

ISBN: 978-0-7643-6443-3

Printed in India

Published by Schiffer Publishing, Ltd.
4880 Lower Valley Road
Atglen, PA 19310
Phone: (610) 593-1777; Fax: (610) 593-2002
Email: Info@schifferbooks.com
Web: www.schifferbooks.com

For our complete selection of fine books on this and related subjects, please visit our website at www.schifferbooks.com. You may also write for a free catalog.

Schiffer Publishing's titles are available at special discounts for bulk purchases for sales promotions or premiums. Special editions, including personalized covers, corporate imprints, and excerpts, can be created in large quantities for special needs. For more information, contact the publisher.

We are always looking for people to write books on new and related subjects. If you have an idea for a book, please contact us at proposals@schifferbooks.com.

Other Schiffer Books by Pat McMillan:
Christmas by Design: Private Homes Decorated by Leading Designers, Patricia Hart McMillan and Katharine Kaye McMillan, ISBN 978-0-7643-5654-4

Christmas at Designers' Homes across America, Katharine Kaye McMillan and Patricia Hart McMillan, ISBN 978-0-7643-5163-1

Christmas at Historic Houses, 2nd ed., Patricia Hart McMillan and Katharine Kaye McMillan, ISBN 978-0-7643-4690-3

And the angel said unto them, Fear not;
for, behold I bring you good tidings of
great joy, which shall be to all people, for
unto you is born this day in the city of
David a Savior, which is Christ the Lord.

Luke 2:10, 11, KJV

Dedicated to Jesus Christ

Contents

REMEMBERING CHRISTMAS
Christopher Radko

Christmas is a day that continues to stay fresh in my mind and heart. As a kid, I recall rushing home from school to do my homework by the light of the Christmas tree. Twinkling, jewel-toned light bulbs cast a kaleidoscope of colors on our living room walls. Bubble lights merrily reflected in the glass spheres and space age ornaments of comets and stars. One of my favorite ornaments was a jolly Santa astride a rocket ship zooming off to the sky. I'd often lay my homework aside and slip under the lowest branches to look up into this pine-scented wonderland. Our Christmas tree was like a portal into a sparkling place of joy-filled peace. Time seemed to stand still, and all was right with the world.

I've carried those memories with me ever since, and decorating for Christmas remains one of my most enjoyed traditions. I am lucky to live in an 1860s stone house with its own memories of many Christmases past. Sometimes I wonder what those celebrations might have been like before the advent of electric lighting. I imagine that my tree stands in the same bay window where previous trees stood more than a century ago, only those were lighted with candles and decorated with homemade creations. And the music—I wonder what carols were sung in this house all those years ago. Today I have a couple hundred vintage Christmas records, some dating to before World War I. Are those songs familiar to the walls of this house? Lately, I have been using vintage ornaments from the '40s, '50s, and '60s to recall my own childhood Christmases.

The Christmas tree is a centerpiece of the holidays, a place for everyone to gather round. The tree is a canvas that reflects our personal traditions and interests. There's no such thing as "wrong" decorating, if it is done from the heart. Christmas ornaments are memory makers, a tangible source for intangible, yet heartfelt feelings. Ornaments connect us to Christmases gone by, and perhaps, to people who are no longer with us. I cherish the few ornaments I still have from when my mom was a little girl in the 1930s.

There's so much more to life than the daily grind. For me, decorating a home is a way of heightening the holidays and creating a welcoming and festive environment for our family

and friends. It's what we do in preparation, but the heart of this holiday is found in reaffirming our connection with friends, family, and our community. It's a time of year when we pause to extend a compassionate hand to others less fortunate. Why can't every day be like Christmas?

I hope you will enjoy this lovely book of homes for the holidays, for all these halls are decked with love. To each and to all, may the spirit of Christmas be in your heart all year through.

 Christopher Radko's re-creations of vintage Christmas tree ornaments have been purchased by collectors worldwide, including the Queen of England. His new company, Heartfully Yours, continues the tradition and benefits many causes: heartfullyyours.com.

Gary Mullis transforms his dining room into the Christopher Radko room with a tree covered entirely in a fabulous collection of Christopher Radko ornaments. *Photos courtesy of Gary E. Mullis, PhD*

TARPLEY - THOMPSON STORE

Reenactors costumed as tradesmen, shopkeepers, and townsfolk.

WILLIAMSBURG STYLE
Colonial Williamsburg

Timeless Colonial Williamsburg—bedrock of American style—always fascinates. But this wonderfully preserved village (known as the Historic Area) is never more enchanting than during the Christmas holidays. Decorations (famously known as "the Williamsburg look") create fresh currents of excitement along Duke of Gloucester Street. Shops, taverns, and homes boast eye-catching wreaths, each outdoing the other in their unique mix of materials, colors, sizes, and shapes. For some, a single spectacular wreath is not enough. In a more-the-merrier mood, evergreen ropes, garlands, and sprays join one or more wreaths in creating a feast for the eye at doors and windows. The effect is one of joyful exuberance.

— WILLIAMSBURG, VIRGINIA —

Wreaths, varied and highly fanciful, contribute to what is known as the Colonial Williamsburg style. They hang on windows, doors, and gates—a source of inspiration for those who love to design their own wreaths. *Photography courtesy the Colonial Williamsburg Foundation*

CHRISTMAS IN COLONIAL TIMES. In the early days, Christmas in Williamsburg was just another day—most often a work day. Businesses and homes were bustling throughout the season. Today, eighty-eight of the village's 500 buildings are original. The others are restorations, built on original foundations or based on an eighteenth-century map—so authentic looking it is difficult to tell that they are not original.

A stroll along the Duke of Gloucester Street, the main thoroughfare, passes the original Margaret Hunter and Taliaferro-Cole shops, and the Prentis Store. Authentically reconstructed buildings include the Pasteur & Galt Apothecary, John Greenhow Store, Raleigh Tavern, and Anderson Blacksmith. Only experts can tell that they are not original structures. As a result, holiday visitors experience village commerce in a way that would have been entirely familiar to colonial-era residents. At the Pasteur and Galt Apothecary Shop, health care products are available from that era. Silversmiths at the Golden Ball Silversmith Shop craft bars of silver into beautiful candlesticks, goblets, hollowware, platters, and a host of other useful and wonderfully decorative household items. Chownings Tavern in the center of town is a convenient spot for a break from strolling and shopping. The menu is colonial-inspired and the Tavern offers its own Old Stitch and Dear Old Mum specialty beers.

 A Colonial Williamsburg evening program, Christmastide at Home, explores how Christmas has been celebrated in Williamsburg through the centuries. It begins with a scene portraying eighteenth-century Christmas customs and then moves to the nineteenth-century holiday in Williamsburg. Dr. Charles Minnigerode, a professor at the College of William and Mary, brought the German tradition of putting up a Christmas tree during the holidays. Minnigerode's tree, adorned with handmade decorations such as popcorn strings, was the first tree in the city and was put up in the St. George Tucker House. The program ends with a depiction of a family celebrating Christmas in Williamsburg during World War II. *Photograph courtesy the Colonial Williamsburg Foundation*

A costumed woman adjusts the cloak of a junior interpreter at the doorway of the Brick House Tavern. *Photography courtesy the Colonial Williamsburg Foundation*

HOMES FOR THE HOLIDAYS. While Christmas at Colonial Williamsburg means exciting events, shopping galore, and fabulous feasting, it also means seeing original homes that exist throughout the historic district. Along the Duke of Gloucester Street are the Taliaferro-Cole, William Lightfoot, Ludwell-Paradise, and James Getty houses.

On Francis Street (which becomes France Street) are imposing private homes, including the Robert Nicolson, Benjamin Waller, and William Finnie houses and the modest Ewing and Orrell houses. Bassett Hall, the unpretentious Williamsburg home of John D. and Amy Aldrich Rockefeller for several weeks each year, is open on occasion. More eye-catching is the Lightfoot House.

Along Nicholson Street, which parallels the main street, one finds notable original homes, including the George Tucker, Tayloe, Coke-Garret, and Peyton-Randolph houses.

 Doorways are often treated to lavish displays of seasonal greenery with the use of wreaths, swags, and garlands. *Photograph courtesy the Colonial Williamsburg Foundation*

MRS. JOHN D. ROCKEFELLER JR., founder of Colonial Williamsburg's Abby Aldrich Rockefeller Folk Art Museum, filled colorful interiors at beautiful Bassett Hall with antiques and early American folk art. One of eighty-eight surviving original houses, it was built between 1753 and 1766 by House of Burgesses' member Philip Johnson. Around 1800, Virginia legislator Burwell Bassett, a nephew of Martha Washington, purchased the house. Rev. Dr. W. A. R. Goodwin, the visionary behind Colonial Williamsburg's restoration, showed the house to philanthropist John D. Rockefeller Jr. in 1926 to pique his interest in funding the ambitious plan. Colonial Williamsburg purchased Bassett Hall in 1927. In 1936 Bassett Hall became home to the Rockefellers while they oversaw the restoration.

 The Peyton Randolph House (dating from 1715), with its distinctive deep red color and holiday decorations, stands out against a background of new-fallen snow at the corner of Nicholson and North England Streets. *Photograph courtesy the Colonial Williamsburg Foundation*

THE STYLISH PEYTON RANDOLPH HOUSE. Of all the houses on Nicholson Street, none is more interesting than the Peyton Randolph house. With its distinctive deep red color, this impressive house consists of three sections joined over the years. The 29-foot-square west wing, built by William Robertson on the corner of Nicholson and North England Streets, dates to 1715. It was sold in 1721 to Sir John Randolph, the only Virginia-born colonist to be knighted by the English crown. Three years later, Randolph bought a lot to the east and built a house on it. Sir John's son, Peyton, inherited the house when he became twenty-four years old. Between the east and west structures, Peyton built a connecting two-story structure with a façade that matched that of the west wing. The 19-square-foot first floor was a parlor. A grand staircase led to a bedroom above that occupied the entire second floor. Peyton and his wife, Betty, opened their home to political activity. Peyton

(whose brother John, a loyalist, had returned to England before the Revolution) was elected to preside over the First Continental Congress.

Alterations to the house included doors to connect the main structure and the west wing. No door was cut through to the east wing. This wing was razed in the nineteenth century and reconstructed by Colonial Williamsburg, which purchased the property in 1938. Restorations to the house occurred in 1939–40 and 1967–68, and it was opened for exhibition in July 1968. Visitors can see fine original walnut wall paneling, handsomely crafted brass door hardware, and original pine floors. And, of course, one will hear about famed guests such as the comte de Rochambeau and the Marquis de Lafayette.

The house is handsome year-round, but especially so during the holidays when winter snow blankets its extensive grounds.

BRUTON PARISH CHURCH
and COLONIAL WILLIAMSBURG

BRUTON PARISH CHURCH is integral to the preserved village of Colonial Williamsburg. An early and major preservation effort, this village emphatically tells the story of the arrival of western culture on the shores of a continent newly discovered by a courageous people. The church is a light, a beacon. The village is a vivid and constant reminder of the importance of preserving historic houses.

The Reverend W. A. R. Goodwin, rector of Bruton Parish Church, provided the vision for the restoration of the historic village. John D. Rockefeller Jr. realized that vision. Today, visitors to the wonderfully preserved town may visit the Bruton Parish Church, the oldest church in the United States. Many of America's founding fathers worshipped in this church. Among men active in the Revolution who attended Bruton Parish Church were Thomas Jefferson, George Washington, Richard Henry Lee, George Wythe, Patrick Henry, and George Mason. The church's history and its cemetery date even earlier.

Today, the holiday visitor to Bruton Parish Church will be treated to an interior beautifully decorated for the Christmas holidays and to concerts of splendid seasonal

 Bruton Parish (Episcopal) Church's history is older than that of Colonial Williamsburg and remains a vital part of that extraordinary village. It was Dr. W. A. R. Goodwin, twice rector of the church and department head at the College of William & Mary, who persuaded John D. Rockefeller Jr. to save Colonial Williamsburg, the amazing example of the early American community that exemplifies the bedrock of the nation's culture. *Photograph courtesy the Colonial Williamsburg Foundation*

 Bruton Parish Church interior at Christmastime. *Photograph courtesy Peter Blankman*

music. But whether one visits in person, via this book, or online, it is easy to express gratitude to Reverend Goodwin by becoming a member of Friends of Bruton. According to church literature, "Friends of Bruton is a worldwide congregation of those who wish to participate in the preservation and promotion of the unique history and spiritual legacy of Bruton Parish Episcopal Church in Colonial Williamsburg." The website www.brutonparish.org/fobowc makes becoming a member quick and easy, and a financial gift to the preservation program is timely in any season.

Christmas garlands and a Della Robbia–style wreath on the front door welcome holiday visitors to the Woodrow Wilson House in Washington, DC. *Photography by Lillis Werder, courtesy President Woodrow Wilson House*

A CAPITAL CHRISTMAS
Woodrow Wilson House

Woodrow Wilson, son and grandson of Presbyterian ministers, was born Christmas week. A devout Christian, in 1913 he became the twenty-eighth president of the United States (1913–1921). Following the 1914 death of President Wilson's wife, gifted artist Ellen Axson, with whom he had three daughters, Wilson married the widowed Edith Bolling Galt, a descendant of Pocahontas, on December 18, 1915. Wilson suffered a paralyzing stroke in 1919 but remained an active president. Near the end of his presidency, Edith chose the house at 2340 S Street, NW, as their home. She considered the four-story, 1916 Georgian Revival house by architect Waddy B. Wood "unpretentious, comfortable, dignified . . . fitted to the needs of a gentleman." Complete with electricity, telephones, and a buzzer system for summoning servants, it was  modern. But to make it more convenient for the ailing Wilson, a lift for carrying trunks to third-floor storage was converted to an elevator. A new exterior driveway entrance allowed easy access to the elevator.

— WASHINGTON, DISTRICT OF COLUMBIA —

A photograph of Woodrow and Edith Wilson in Paris sits on a foyer side table decorated with a spray of holiday greenery.

A view from the doorway of the gracious foyer with its period-style furnishings and impressive bronze statue. Poinsettias decorate this first-floor foyer. House curators say that Edith Wilson used red poinsettias to decorate the table at the White House and probably used them to decorate her home on S Street, too.

The Wilsons moved into the S Street house in 1921. To date, President Wilson was the only president to have made Washington his permanent home following his term in office. About 90 percent of the furnishings and memorabilia on view in the house belonged to the Wilsons during their occupancy. Among them is the grandfather clock on the stair landing. Edith wanted Wilson to feel at home in their new quarters, so she had Wilson's favorite White House grandfather clock replicated. She also had Wilson's bed custom-designed to replicate the dimensions of the bed he used while in the White House. Wilson lived at S Street for three years until his death in 1924. Edith gave the house to the National Trust for Historic Preservation in 1956. She continued living there until her death in 1961.

 The drawing room includes an intimate seating group. Above the mantle is *L'Esperance,* a painting by artist Hovsep Pushman, presented to President Wilson at the White House on November 27, 1917, by an Armenian delegation on behalf of the artist's wife. There is also a mosaic of the repentance of Saint Peter, given to President Wilson in 1919 by Pope Benedict XV at the Vatican. Near the Steinway and Sons grand piano is a Gobelin tapestry, a gift from the French government to the Wilsons in 1917.

CHRISTMAS ON S STREET. How did the Wilsons celebrate Christmas in their new home? Associate manager and curator Stephanie Daugherty describes the scene then and now:

The Wilsons had a Della Robbia-style wreath on the front door and a big tree with electric lights in the solarium. They received many flowers as gifts, particularly roses, that filled the house. We decorate the house today as it would have been during the Wilsons' residency. Remember that red and green were common, but not exclusive, colors for decorating. For Christmas 2014, we used a palette that Edith might have enjoyed.

Paper novelties were very fashionable and readily available through Dennison's Manufacturing Co. and local stores. Crepe paper printed with winter scenes could be pinned to a table skirt or pasted to roller shades. Dennison's printed special supplements showing how to create crepe paper wreaths, garlands, party favors, lamp shades, and even a crepe paper fireplace and mantel. Today, crepe paper and greenery trail down from a mantelpiece in typical 1920s style. Fireplaces were seldom used except for ambience, so there was little danger of fire.

Edith welcomed Woodrow to their new home with a replica of his favorite White House tall case (grandfather) clock. The clock stands on the staircase landing near the Palladian window, which reflects lights from the Christmas tree. Even the clock's intricate face is decorated for the holidays.

Another well-established Christmas tradition is arranging little villages around the nativity or under the Christmas tree. During the nineteenth century, people began putting cardboard candy boxes in these Christmas villages. As electric Christmas lights became more affordable, the cardboard candy boxes transitioned to ornaments for the tree. The paper houses had small holes in the back to insert an electric light. We have excellent examples of these "fairy/glitter/putz" cardboard houses on our tree and on the top portion of the side buffet.

Typically, unwrapped large and bulky toys for children might be placed under the tree on Christmas Eve, with smaller gifts, wrapped or unwrapped, actually on the tree branches. Although printed wrapping paper started being used in 1917, it was still uncommon in the early 1920s. The Wilsons used colored tissue or crepe paper with plain or printed ribbon and seals (stickers). Scotch tape was not invented until 1930, so narrow ribbon or tape was tied decoratively. Artificial flowers, leaves, seals, and the ever-present good luck holly sprig were often used to decorate packages.

Next to Wilson's desk in the library, mail bags stuffed with letters and packages represent the volume of mail—thousands of letters and telegrams—received for Christmas, his birthday, and New Year's. All were acknowledged. So a good portion of Wilson's day was taken up with correspondence during the holidays, whether he wrote letters himself or dictated to his personal secretary, John Randolph Bolling. Also in the library, on December 6, 1922, French premier George Clemenceau came for tea at 5:30 p.m.

The Wilsons celebrated Christmas (both here and at the White House) with a family dinner in the evening, followed by the exchange of gifts in the library or at the table. Margaret (Wilson's eldest daughter), Dr. Axson, John Randolph Bolling (Wilson's personal secretary and brother-in-law), Mrs. W. H. Bolling (Edith's mother), and Bertha (Edith's sister) were usually the guests. For Christmas 2014, the table was set for dinner in a similar manner as it would have been on Christmas Day 1922.

In 1922, Christmas season was a happy time. Wilson's health was noticeably improved and there

 During the holidays, the dining room looks much as it did when the Wilsons were at home here. A modern interpretation of Christmas dinner at the Wilson's house in 1922 sets the table with the Martha Washington china, silverware, and glasses that are part of the collection belonging to the house. Flowers are a simple but colorful arrangement. Ribbon candy is beautifully displayed on the buffet. A portrait of Edith Wilson painted by Seymour Stone hangs over the richly carved decorative mantel in the dining room. Lush seasonal greenery, fruit, and ribbon add a note of Christmas.

were frequent small dinner parties. The Wilsons dressed for dinner, which began at 6:00 p.m. While we don't know exactly which set of china the Wilsons used, we have set the table with the "Martha Washington" pattern. This is an early-twentieth-century reproduction of a design made for Martha Washington in 1796. This reproduction set was a 1915 wedding gift to the Wilsons from Mr. and Mrs. Nathan Straus of New York. The design features the names of fifteen states (there were fifteen states in the Union in 1796) enclosed in an endless chain guarded by a serpent that symbolizes perpetuity. The Latin phrase in the center translates: "Honour and Protection from this." Place cards for

dinner attendees included Mr. Wilson, Edith, Margaret, Edith's mother and sister, John Randolph Bolling, and Dr. Stockton Axson. The glasses, utensils, and nut bowls used to set the table are all from the Wilsons' personal collection. We know that Edith used poinsettias on the table at the White House and she may also have done so on S Street. (Only red poinsettias were available until the 1960s.) Table favors were very popular—small gifts, "crackers" or paper novelties. These were frequently attached to ribbons that could be pulled to the recipient's place.

Dinner almost certainly included oysters, turkey, and other game birds that Wilson received as gifts from his many friends and admirers. All the traditional Christmas desserts such as plum pudding and fruitcake were popular then as today. On the sideboards are desserts common in the 1920s, including ribbon candy, peppermints, and coconut snowballs. According to *My Memoir* by Mrs. Edith Wilson, "After dinner the table was cleared and the gifts brought in and opened. We let the servants go, and spent most of the evening around the board…" (The 2014 interpretation included some gifts in the dining room as well as in the library since these are the places the Wilsons opened gifts while living at the house.)

Among notable gifts received for Christmas 1922 was a moving picture from the MacAdoo family of their new house in California and Wilson's two granddaughters. Subtitles were produced by William MacAdoo's friend, Douglas Fairbanks Sr. and his production company.

All was merry and bright on Christmas 1922, as the holidays are today at the house on S Street.

 Opposite page
This modern Christmas tree stands in the same place as it did during the Wilsons' time in residence. Guests arriving downstairs were greeted to a prominent view of this beautiful tree with electric lights through the Palladian window on the staircase. Traditional decorations for the Wilson House Christmas trees include a miniature nativity scene and a modern example of a *putz* or holiday village. There is also a modern paper dove and a tiny church building made of paper, following a popular trend in the 1920s.

 A sweeping view of the handsome library/study was visible from Wilson's desk. His portrait by Stanislav Rembski hangs over the decorated mantel.

 A bookshelf in the third-floor hallway is treated to Christmas decorations, including a big red ribbon.

Second Inauguration
of
Woodrow Wilson
President of the United States
and
Thomas Riley Marshall
Vice President of the United States

March 5, 1917

Architects Carrère & Hastings worked closely with Gertrude Pitcairn to create a residence that is both impressive in scale and welcoming in impression. *Photograph courtesy Cairnwood Estates*

GILDED AGE GATHERING
Cairnwood Estate

America's Gilded Age was about more than mere glitter. Cairnwood, the grand Beaux Arts country home of John and Gertrude Pitcairn, dazzles; but the eye is drawn to the distinctive tower that houses the family chapel. It is visual testimony to the fact that Christ, the central figure in Christmas, figured significantly in the inspiring lives of this devout couple, who were prominent contributors to the Bryn Athyn community, the Bryn Athyn Cathedral, the Academy of the New Church, and Bryn Athyn College.

John Pitcairn, a Scottish immigrant and cofounder of Pittsburgh Plate Glass, lived at Cairnwood with his family from its construction in 1895 until his death in 1916. "On Christmas Day, the family would go to church in the morning, and in the afternoon Cairnwood was opened to the community to celebrate," says Lisa Parker-Adams, director of history and education at Cairnwood.

— BRYN ATHYN, PENNSYLVANIA —

 The entry to Cairnwood, ablaze with lights, welcomes guests to Christmas festivities.
Photography by Rachel Kathryn

We know something about how the holidays were celebrated through the memoirs of Viola Heath Ridgeway, a maid who began living there with her sister Flora sometime before 1921. Viola was born in 1898 and moved to Bryn Athyn with her family shortly after the turn of the century. Her theatrical parents founded a theater company and directed plays on the Cairnwood grounds. Records show that Mrs. Pitcairn often hired church members as live-in staff, recruiting help through a widely distributed journal called *New Church Life*. Viola's memoir about the early days in the community, *The Old Houses*, recalls Christmas celebrations at Cairnwood.

There were the gay Christmas gatherings, when everyone in the community would be invited. The brightness and warmth of the home with huge logs burning in all the fireplaces and Mr. Pitcairn standing there with his beaming smile and his hearty handshake greeting his guests, was a scene of joy never to be forgotten. . . . Mr. Pitcairn didn't forget the children, for each small hand that he shook found a shiny fifty cent piece lying in his palm. Oh, this was wealthy to them! The huge Christmas tree that stood in the court area and reached up to the railing of the gallery on the second floor, as the day grew dark, was lit with what seemed to the small people thousands of candles.

Family members recall Christmas as a time of parental generosity. Lisa Parker-Adams shared what the Pitcairns' son Theodore wrote about his childhood memories.

The two days of the year which stand out strongest in my childhood memory were Christmas Day and Founders Day which was on the 14th of January. At about three o'clock on Christmas afternoon, the Starkey clan arrived at Cairnwood; Aunty Sophie told stories and we all sang Christmas carols. Father had piles of twenty, ten and five dollar gold pieces on his desk, and everyone went to get their gold piece according to their age. All then went in a procession to supper in the dining room, singing "Merry Christmas Bells Are Ringing." After supper the younger children went home, and the rest of the evening was given over to music.

To visit Cairnwood at any time of the year is to marvel at the amazing legacy of a Gilded Age couple who looked beyond self to the welfare of their family, their community of believers, and ultimately to posterity. Their home and surrounding grounds and buildings were created with the greatest of care. According to Parker-Adams, "The architects of Cairnwood, Carrère & Hastings were trained at the famous École des Beaux Arts—The School of Fine Arts—in Paris in the early 1880s. Like the grand English and French country houses, Cairnwood was designed to graciously accommodate a wide variety of social occasions inside and out. Three generations of Pitcairns living in Cairnwood entertained often, hosting plays, musical concerts, dinners, and dances for the community throughout the year. Keeping pace with a growing community, after John Pitcairn died in 1916, the Christmas guest list was revised to include only immediate family and cousins." Today, the grand house is once again open to the public.

Cairnwood has always been lavishly decorated for the holidays. Director Shannon Walko notes, "Historic photographs ca. 1923 show a two-story Christmas tree in the Parlor Hall. It was decorated with glass balls and tinsel. Electric lights replaced the traditional candles used at the turn of the century. Today our 20-foot Christmas tree stands in its traditional place in the great hall, adorned with more than 3,000 white lights, 300 pieces of sugared fruit, and gold glass ornaments."

Ropes of greenery were woven together with special vines and flowers grown in the estate green houses to furnish the decorations for holidays and special occasions. Historic photographs show that roping was draped from the second-floor gallery and wound down the stairs, around windows, and over every mantel.

"During the 1920s and '30s, the Pitcairn children hung their stockings by the fireplace in the boudoir, the sitting room on the second floor adjoining with suites of family bedrooms," Walko says.

The senior Pitcairns exchanged Christmas cards. "Every year John and Gertrude Pitcairn designed custom Christmas and New Year cards," she says. "We have several examples of cards from the 1880s and '90s. My favorite one is a pale blue Christmas and New Year greeting from 1890. It is simple and modern in comparison to the more typical Victorian style" A selection of Christmas cards from the archives is on display during the annual Cairnwood by Candlelight holiday event.

This event enhances the feeling of returning to the Gilded Age at Christmas. The house is filled with live music, sumptuous Yuletide treats are on offer, and tour guides are dressed in period fashions. Gowns and party dresses that belonged to three generations of Pitcairn women (1870s–1950s) are displayed throughout the bedrooms. This extensive exhibition continues throughout December.

Festive Holiday Tea & Tours offer guests a traditional three-course English tea served throughout the grand first floor. Tours of the decorated rooms and service wing on the second and third floors follow. The Children's Tea with Santa is popular with families, who are given souvenir professional photographs taken beside the Christmas tree.

For those who cannot visit Cairnwood at Christmastime, a permanent Cairnwood Family Gallery opened recently in the former Playroom on the third floor. Furniture, books, photographs, artifacts, and some of the children's toys, baby furniture, and dresses are on display year-round.

 Evening lighting at Cairnwood by Candlelight plays up the stonework details of this grand country house designed for a wide variety of social occasions. *Photograph courtesy Cairnwood Estates*

 At night, triple arched doorways that open directly onto a gracious terrace become the focal point of the exterior. *Photograph courtesy Shea Roggio Photography*

Inside the intimate family chapel, the Hebrew inscription above the altar is translated as "Hear, O Israel: The Lord our God, the Lord is One! You shall love the Lord your God with all your heart, with all your soul, and with all your might." Deuteronomy 6:4–5. *Photograph courtesy of Candid Moments Photography*

An octagonal dome covers the small space. *Photograph courtesy Allure West Studios*

 Mantels and floral displays throughout the house are distinctively decorated by area florists. Christmas 2020 participating florists included Off Shoots Décor, Fleur De Lis Florals, Precious Petals, Robertson's Flowers, and Posey Hill Flowers. *Photography by Candid Moments*

The Great Hall and terrace are a prime area for entertaining. The huge Cairnwood Christmas tree is a focal point during the holiday season. *Photography courtesy Candid Moments Photography*

Top

In the library, Gertrude Starkey Pitcairn's formal gown is worn with a black-silk cut-velvet mantle, an evening wrap with both jacket and cape features to accommodate the gown's bustle silhouette. *Photography by Rachel Kathryn*

Left

The 1930s silk velvet formal evening coat trimmed in white fox fur was made for Gabriel Pitcairn Pendleton. *Photography courtesy of Cairnwood Estate*

Middle

A mink-trimmed pink brocade coat was created for Jill Pendleton, daughter of Gabriel Pitcairn Pendleton. *Photography courtesy of Cairnwood Estate*

Right

Lisa Parker-Adams, Cairnwood director of history and education, wears an 1870s-style ball gown she made, inspired by the green velvet 1889 bustle gown from the Pitcairn Collection. *Photography courtesy of Cairnwood Estate*

 Clockwise from top left
On the second floor, the triple-arched balustrade overlooks the Great Hall. Archway openings are accentuated with lighted topiaries in handsome urns. Guest rooms line this second-floor gallery. *Photograph courtesy Candid Moments Photography*

Kathrine Stelzer, Temple University history intern, poses in an 1870s reproduction dress that she sewed. She co-curated the Cairnwood by Candlelight exhibit in 2010. *Photograph courtesy Candid Moments Photography*

Teams of guides and volunteers wear period costumes representing various historical decades at the Cairnwood by Candlelight festivities. Left to right: Lisa Parker-Adams, Christine McDonald, Teka Echols, Carol Henderson, Tania Buss, Clara Huntzinger, Gwenda Cowley, Tara Fehon, Becca Uber, Shannon Walko. *Photograph courtesy Candid Moments Photography*

 Opposite, clockwise from top
In the Yellow Room, one of three guest rooms at the head of the stairs on the second floor, is a dress that belonged to Vera Pitcairn, only daughter in the family. *Dress collection courtesy Glencairn Museum. Photography courtesy Candid Moments Photography*

In a guest room adjoining the Yellow Room is Gertrude Pitcairn's oak partner desk with a matching carved book shelf. John Pitcairn is believed to have used the desk and bookshelf in his study adjoining the first-floor library. The exhibited dress (courtesy the Glencairn Museum), ca. 1883–1888, was likely an at-home dress. *Photograph courtesy Candid Moments Photography*

A gold and cream porcelain teapot by Haviland & Co., Limoges, France. The cream, gold, and green porcelain sugar bowl and cream pitcher are by Wm. Guérin & Co., Limoges, France. *Photograph courtesy Candid Moments Photography*

Clockwise from top left
The little boy's velvet suit and silk shirt were hand-sewn by Jean Jungé Studios, run by three sisters in Glenview, Illinois, and members of the New Church there. They traveled to Bryn Athyn regularly to collect and deliver custom orders. *Photograph courtesy Candid Moments Photography*

The boudoir in the 1920s and '30s served as a private living room. It was also the place where dress fittings took place with Mrs. Edelman of H. Odhner Edleman, Paris & New York (who designed dresses for daughter-in-law Mildred). On display is a child's peach silk velveteen dress and bonnet, ca. 1920s and '30s, possibly purchased in France. The label reads Miguapouf, 12 Rue Boissy D'Anglas, Paris. *Photograph courtesy Candid Moments Photography*

THE STORY OF SCOTLAND-BORN JOHN PITCAIRN, as told in the brochure *Cairnwood, A Home In The Country*, is that of America's ideal self-made man. At age five, he came with his parents to Pittsburgh, where he and his family were baptized in the New Church (founded by Swedish scientist, philosopher, and theologian Emanuel Swedenborg). In 1855, at age fourteen, Pitcairn left home with a knapsack that held a Bible and Emanuel Swedenborg's "True Christian Religion." He took a job as a telegraph operator, worked his way to superintendent of a Pennsylvania Railroad branch, and became wealthy by investing in coal, oil, and gas. Cofounder of the Pittsburgh Plate Glass company, Pitcairn was board chairman at his death at age seventy-five. We read that Pitcairn, who had made his fortune in the age of robber barons, "had earned a reputation for fair play and the highest personal character."

The Pitcairns' love story is one of exactitude on her part and perseverance on his. Gertrude Starkey was also a member of the New Church, which teaches that marriage is for eternity. When the thirty-eight-year-old Pitcairn asked the twenty-four-year-old Gertrude to marry him, she declined. They had been acquainted for only two years. John's persistence won and five years later, in the fall of 1883, she accepted. They were married in January 1884.

 The living room—largest room in the western wing—is finished in original black walnut paneling and rich red brocade-style wallpaper. Over the fireplace is a portrait of Dr. George Starkey, Gertrude's father, who graduated from the Homeopathic Medical College of Pennsylvania, Philadelphia, in 1855. The coral silk velvet jacket with wide fur collar, ca. 1920s, likely belonged to Gabriele Pitcairn Pendleton, born in Cairnwood in 1913, the daughter of Raymond and Mildred Pitcairn. Gabriele was the last family owner of Cairnwood. *Photograph courtesy Candid Moments Photography*

 The *boudoir*, on the sunny side of the house, was a sitting room for the lady of the house. French doors open onto a balcony with spectacular views of the farmland. Period clothing was part of a special exhibit. *Photograph courtesy Candid Moments Photography*

For eleven years, John and Gertrude lived in Philadelphia, where five of their six children were born. During that time, the Pitcairns and members of the New Church began to talk about moving to the country for a healthier environment for their children. In 1889, the Pitcairns purchased farmland in Huntingdon Valley and church members began commuting to the area for worship services. Later, the Pitcairns bought 550 acres for the church community and a school. In 1893, plans for the community settlement were drawn up by Charles Eliot of Olmsted, Olmsted, and Eliot, a landscape architecture firm. (A principal member, Frederick Law Olmsted, is considered the father of American landscape design.) It was time to consider building a home in the country for John and Gertrude Pitcairn and their children.

CAIRNWOOD, NEW HOME *for* THE PITCAIRNS

JOHN AND GERTRUDE PITCAIRN looked to Carrère and Hastings, a New York City architectural and planning firm known for grand institutions (the New York Public Library) to design their new home. The Paris-trained partners worked with Gertrude Pitcairn to create a chateau-like Beaux Arts residence with a striking octagonal tower that contains a family chapel. Work began in 1892 and was completed in spring 1895.

Not all architect-client collaborations are satisfying, but Cairnwood proved that they can be. After visiting the furnished home, architect Thomas Hastings wrote a letter to his hostess telling her how much he had appreciated her intelligent interest in the project. He told her that "so much is dependent upon the good taste and judgment of the client that the architect oftimes [sic] suffers—when he is not really responsible." He couldn't resist the impulse, he told her, to write and tell her how pleased he was to see the great improvements she had accomplished. This was a high compliment from one of the world's leading architects.

The large three-story residence, garden house, greenhouses, pergola, and stables together with courtyard, gardens, and surrounding farmland constituted a country estate. Gertrude enjoyed this magnificent house for three years before

 Ornate oak dining room sideboard and chairs are displayed on the second floor gallery, while the original table completing the set is in the Cairnwood family gallery on the third floor. *Photograph courtesy Candid Moments Photography*

her death in 1898. John, convinced that marriage was for eternity, never remarried. He reared his three sons and daughter at Cairnwood and lived there until his death in July 1916.

The Pitcairns' eldest son, Raymond, his wife Mildred, and their family lived at Cairnwood until their home, Glencairn, was completed next door in 1939. Cairnwood remained unoccupied until the end of World War II, when Raymond's daughter Gabriele, her husband the Rev. Willard Pendleton, and their family moved in. The Pendletons lived there until 1980, when both Cairnwood and Glencairn were given to the Academy of the New Church.

Cairnwood remained empty for a decade or more before a restoration managed by John Milner Architects was completed in 1994 and the house opened to the public in 1995. It was designated a National Historic Landmark in 2008—part of the Athyn Historic District, comprised of Cairnwood, the remarkable Glencairn Museum, and the inspiring Bryn Athyn Cathedral.

Beneath a Christmas tree are a replica rocking horse (*left*) and a 1920s wooden horse (*right*) from the family collections. *Photograph courtesy Candid Moments Photography*

Musical concerts enliven holiday events at Cairnwood. Here performers are in a handsome room connected to the living room by sliding pocket doors. Furnished in white American oak, bookshelves feature storage and built-in tables. When visiting this room, look for the bronze reliefs on either side of the fireplace (not shown). They are fashioned after the "Fountain of the Innocents" (Jean Goujon) and cast by the foundry of Ferdinand Barbedienne (1810–1892). A portrait of John Pitcairn by August Benziger, 1908, hangs above the fireplace (not shown). *Photography courtesy Candid Moments Photography*

Small decorative touches throughout this grand house delight the senses. *Photography courtesy Candid Moments Photography*

Opposite
This 1823 federal and Greek revival house in Lowell, Massachusetts, home to four key figures in America's Industrial Revolution, is a museum dedicated to the work of its most famous resident, the artist James McNeill Whistler. *Photography by Caroline Gallaher, courtesy O'Connor Studio*

ART FOR CHRISTMAS
Whistler House

What would Whistler think—his birthplace a museum, main rooms galleries! The Lowell Art Association made James McNeill Whistler's birthplace the Association's permanent home in 1908. Established in 1878 as the Lowell Art Association, it is the oldest incorporated art association in the United States and is known internationally for its distinguished collection of nineteenth- and early-twentieth-century New England representational art. The association owns and operates the Whistler House Museum of Art as a historic site that represents the richness of the history and art of Lowell. The Whistler House hosts many exhibits, lectures, concerts, educational and community programs, and an array of social events in the residence, gallery, and adjoining Victorian park.

— LOWELL, MASSACHUSETTS —

SARA M. BOGOSIAN, president of the Whistler House Museum of Art, says, "Sometimes amid our daily activities, it is easy to forget how critical the arts are to our lives. The truth is that they give us balance. Just like other types of learning, knowledge of art and creative expression and thinking leads to a life of fulfillment and accomplishment, giving us a foundation for meeting today's social challenges." Under Bogosian's direction, the museum maintains a permanent art collection, organizes contemporary and historical fine art exhibitions, and sponsors educational and community-oriented cultural programs. The museum is a beehive of activity year-round, but perhaps never more so than during the Christmas season.

 The stairway in the main foyer and museum entry is decorated with garlands for the Christmas season. The portrait is of David Neal, former president of the Lowell Art Association, the oldest incorporated art association in the United States, which owns and operates the Whistler House Museum of Art.

 Above the mantel in the Francis Room hangs a portrait of former house resident James Bicheno Francis, inventor of the belt-driven turbine.

 Edith Fairfax Davenport's original painting *Apres James McNeill Whistler, Arrangement in Grey and Black* hangs in the Francis Room (named for James Bicheno Francis, former resident known as the father of modern hydraulic engineering). It is a copy of Whistler's original painting, *Arrangement in Grey and Black, No. 1*, which hangs in the Musée D'Orsay in Paris.

 To the left of the mantel in the Francis Room hangs a portrait of Thomas Bailey Lawson of the Lowell Art Association. The Christmas tree and an eggnog-filled punch bowl greet holiday visitors.

The handsome three-story, fourteen-room house combines federal and Greek revival architectural elements including Greek Revival cornice returns and a third-story Palladian window on the side elevation. The five-bay façade—a dignified study in gray and black—is classically symmetrical, with pairs of six-over-six double-hung windows flanking a holiday wreath-decorated central door with sidelights. Tall chimneys punctuate the corners of the structure, which contains ten fireplaces.

Built in 1823, this house was home to four men who were key figures in America's Industrial Revolution. While it is not likely that the house would have become a museum dedicated to any one of them, it is good to know about these distinguished residents whose lives were devoted to the industrial arts. Briefly:

1823–1831. Paul Moody, with Francis Cabot Lowell, created America's first power loom, revolutionizing America's textile industry, since young females could operate these high-speed machines.

1834–1837. Major George Washington Whistler (father of the painter), a West Point graduate, resigned from the Army in 1833, to become one of the most famous engineers in the United States. He designed canals, aqueducts, locomotives (the first with a steam whistle), and the first keystone arch railroad bridge (intact and in service), and laid out "impossible" railway routes. Tsar Nicholas I of Russia hired Major Whistler to build a railroad between St. Petersburg and Moscow. Whistler moved his family (wife Anna, their two sons James and Williams, and his three children by his deceased first wife) from this house to Russia. It was in Russia that his son, James, enrolled in an art school—the first step in his remarkable career.

1837–1845. George Brownell authored *Journal on a Voyage to England* in 1839, while living in the house. As superintendent of the Lowell Machine Shops, Brownell traveled to England, the world's leading industrial nation, to order machinery to be shipped home to Lowell. He also looked at industrial premises—some say as an industrial spy.

1845–1869. English-born James Bicheno Francis, an engineer, became known as the father of modern hydraulic engineering. His biography is well worth reading.

The main gallery features a beautiful hand-painted eighteenth-century grandfather clock, and the dining room exhibits paintings from the nineteenth- and twentieth-century collection.

WHISTLER, THE ARTIST. Of all the residents of 243 Worthen Street, the most famous is Whistler, the painter. Born on July 11, 1834, he was christened James Abbott Whistler at St. Anne's Episcopal Church. After his mother's death, he dropped the name Abbott and included McNeill, his mother's maiden name, in his signature. His biography is a fascinating tale of his journey from childhood sketching to the creation of a work that all seem to know—his *Arrangement in Grey and Black, No. 1* (known as "Whistler's Mother").

Whistler had always loved drawing. At age nine he enrolled in the Imperial Academy of Fine Arts in St. Petersburg, Russia, where his father was designing and building a railroad between Moscow and St. Petersburg. About that time, in 1844, noted artist Sir William Allan saw Whistler's drawings and advised his mother that her son had considerable genius but should not be pushed beyond his natural inclinations. When her husband died of cholera at age forty-eight, Anna Whistler and her children returned to Connecticut, where she enrolled young James in a school that would prepare him for a career as a minister. That was not a good fit, so Whistler entered his father's alma mater, the United States Military Academy at West Point in 1851, where Robert E. Lee was superintendent. Young Whistler's sketches of cadets were very clever and his grades for (engineering) drawing classes excellent, but he failed chemistry. Reportedly, he said, "Were silicon a gas, I would have been a general." But silicon was not a gas, Whistler was not happy, and he departed. He knocked about, spent some time in Baltimore and decided in 1855 to head for Paris. Over the next twenty-two years, he moved back and forth between Paris and London (considered his home), a part of the community of noted artists in both cities. He traveled to Chile and spent time in Venice, where he developed etching skills. His etchings have been declared the best since Rembrandt.

 The historic kitchen, with its beehive oven, has an authentic 1858 stove and icebox.

 A magnificent painting hangs above each of the ten fireplaces in the Whistler House.

61

In 1861, Whistler's *Symphony in White, No. 1* ("The White Girl") created a great deal of interest. Ten years later, in 1871, he decided to paint a portrait of his mother. Entitled *Arrangement in Grey and Black, No. 1*, this is considered one of the four most recognizable American paintings. (The other three are *American Gothic* by Grant Wood, *Nighthawks* by Edward Hopper, and *Campbell Soup Can* by Andy Warhol.) The painting of his mother created much controversy in the art world and marked Whistler as an early modernist painter. Controversial as it was, the French government purchased the painting for the Musée du Luxembourg in 1891. It was the first painting by an American to hang in this venerable museum. Today, it hangs in the Musée D'Orsay in Paris.

Whistler is extolled for elevating the everyday to a high level of beauty. One critic says that he can easily spot professional imitations of Whistler's work because it is *beautiful*. His "moonlights" (night scapes), renamed "nocturnes" by a musical friend, are wonderful examples of the ordinary becoming extraordinary. *Nocturne: Blue and Gold—Old Battersea Bridge* (1872), hangs in the Tate Britain in London. In this painting, line (once very important) seems to be in the act of dissolving, as though the artist has captured the very moment when matter becomes spirit, with viewer as witness.

Whistler, it is said, did not consider himself an American painter. But America claims him, and Lowell is delighted to point out that he is a native son.

 The statue of James McNeill Whistler in Whistler Park is by Mico Kaufman.

THE PERMANENT COLLECTION on DISPLAY

The Museum's permanent collection focuses on late nineteenth and early-twentieth-century American representational art, mainly by New England artists. Here are key works.

Silver trays and a delightful topiary decorate the elegant butler's pantry.

THE FRANCIS ROOM
James B. Francis, by R. M. Staigg
Apres James McNeill Whistler, Arrangement in Grey and Black (1906), oil on canvas, by Edith Fairfax Davenport, a cousin of Whistler, an exact-scale copy of the original painting.
Lowell in 1825, by Benjamin Mather
Rev. Theodore Edison, 1875, by Thomas Bayley Lawson

THE MAIN GALLERY
The Children, by Frank W. Benson
Philip Marden, by Marie Danforth Page
Portrait of Woman in Profile, by Mary Earl Wood

SECOND FLOOR
Annie Seated (1858), *The Pool* (1859), *The Old Rag Woman* (1859), *Bibi Lalouette* (1859); etchings by James McNeill Whistler

Fonthill, a concrete castle ca. 1908–1912, borrows liberally from medieval, Gothic, and Byzantine styles. The realized fantasy of Henry Chapman Mercer, the building is a showcase for the Arts and Crafts ceramic tiles manufactured by his Moravian Pottery and Tile Works. Tiles decorating the risers of entry steps read "except the Lord build…"
Photography by Carla Klouda, courtesy Carla Klouda Photography

A CHRISTMAS CASTLE
Fonthill Museum

Fonthill is every child's impression of a castle. The façade's somewhat higgildy-piggildy look is a dead giveaway to the fact that the structure grew without architectural plans, satisfying the owner/designer's creative urge. Seemingly haphazardly placed windows neither match nor align—a clue that symmetry, balance, and rhythm lagged behind other criteria. Indeed, Mercer is said to have designed the building room-by-room, inside-out, with the exterior an afterthought. Little wonder that the spectacular façade of Fonthill fascinates, and that the interior of this unique blend of medieval, Gothic, and Byzantine styles is a visual feast.

Fonthill's owner—Henry Chapman Mercer, a "jack-of-all-trades" and master of many—built his poured-in-place concrete castle between 1908 and 1912 with money left to him by a wealthy aunt who died in 1905. The labyrinth-like floor plan contains thirty-two stairways, twenty-one chimneys, forty-four rooms (ten were bathrooms), eighteen fireplaces, and an amazingly eclectic assortment of some 200 windows with views of his surrounding 66 acres of beautiful grounds.

— DOYLESTOWN, PENNSYLVANIA —

Gray concrete walls in the Columbus Room are a quiet foil for brilliant red Christmas decorations. Tiles cover the interior of arched niches.

A glowing Christmas tree brightens the multi-level entry hall with its elaborately decorated ceiling.

In the lavishly embellished structure, Mercer (an archeologist) adorned the walls with ceramics and artifacts collected in his world travels, as gifts, and through his own collecting. These include Mesopotamian cuneiform tablets dating back to 2063 BCE.

Fonthill was a showplace for the handcrafted arts and crafts style ceramic tiles made in Mercer's own Moravian Pottery and Tile Works factory just a short walk from his home. At Fonthill, the fireplaces, built-in furniture, walls, and ceilings were opportunities to show off his tiles, some of which are Gothic in theme, all of which are captivating. Today, some handmade reissues of tiles and mosaics can be ordered from the Moravian

Pottery and Tile Works. A National Historic Landmark, it is maintained as a "working history" museum by Pennsylvania's Bucks County Department of Parks and Recreation. Tiles made in this factory are still handmade much as they were when Mercer directed it from 1898 until his death in 1930.

Mercer's tiles are on display in such famous places as Kykuit, the Rockefeller estate in Pocantico Hills, New York; Grauman's Chinese Theater in Hollywood, California, and the Casino at Monte Carlo, Monaco. The largest installation of Mercer's tiles is found on the floor of the Pennsylvania State Capitol Building in Harrisburg, in which 400 mosaic tiles depict Pennsylvania flora, fauna, and history from prehistoric times to the early twentieth century.

 Tiles on the concrete desktop, stairway walls,
and arches convey an impression of
controlled exuberance.

Seasonal greenery adorns one of the eighteen fireplaces in Fonthill, notable for its sedate size, gently arched opening, and cobalt-blue accent tiles.

The tree's amber lights echo the drapery color in this small room outfitted with beautiful cabinetry. Ceiling arches are articulated with tiles from the Mercer Pottery and Tile Works.

company. The factory was completed in 1912.

Mercer was one of the archaeologists and paleontologists who investigated the Port Kennedy Bone Cave, which held one of the most important middle Ice Age fossil deposits in the United States. The cave is in the boundaries of Valley Forge National Park.

Known also for his research, Mercer amassed 6,000 books (many with marginalia and indexes added by him) covering a wide range of subjects including ceramic tile, architecture, ancient tools, and literature. His astounding collection of early American tools is housed in the Mercer Museum, which he built a mile from Fonthill. Henry Ford declared this to be the only museum worth visiting in the US.

Mercer did send and receive gifts at Christmastime, and even made his own greeting cards. However, "An entry in his diary for Saturday, December 22, 1928, indicates that Mercer, a bachelor, may have treated Christmas as just another day, a day to work and be accomplished," says Gayle Shupack of the Bucks County Historical Society. "He wrote: 'Gloomy Christmas relieved by making 2 more styles for tree labels. This morning also devised 2 wire springs . . . to hold together ends of wire-net sleeve around tree trunks . . . thus perfecting not only the labels, but their method of suspension without bark contact & with allowance for trunk expansion. This week also finished Index for Ancient Carpenters' Tools & sent it off to Dr. Dow . . . sent silhouette drawing for figure using brace & bit—for the other cover side of the bound book."

Fonthill Castle is far from gloomy at Christmastime today. The halls and rooms are decked with Victorian-style decorations and numerous Christmas trees that remain on display throughout the season. On two Saturdays in December, after-hours events include a ticketed, reservations-only holiday lights tour by candlelight. Refreshments are served. All is merry and bright!

A Doylestown native, Mercer earned a liberal arts degree at Harvard University (1875–1879), and a law degree at University of Pennsylvania Law School (1880–1881), and was admitted to the Philadelphia County Bar (November 1881). Instead of practicing law, he traveled in Europe and around the Mediterranean (1881–1904). In the early 1890s he was appointed curator of American and prehistoric archaeology at the University of Pennsylvania Museum. In the late 1890s, he left to devote himself to searching for old American artifacts. He studied German redware pottery, apprenticed himself to a Pennsylvania German potter, and in 1898, founded his tile

During the holidays, house and gardens glitter with miles of lights and thousands of ornaments. The entry courtyard display, new each season, is always a showstopper. *Except where noted, photography by Ned Gault, courtesy of Ned T. Gault Photography / Mente Serano, California*

A COUNTRY HOUSE CHRISTMAS
Filoli

Filoli's gracious country house is carefully sited amidst 16 acres of formal gardens with reflecting pools, arbors, and shady walks that blend serenely with the Santa Cruz Mountains. Surrounded by the 654-acre estate, the grand house and its well-tended grounds comprise one of California's finest remaining country estates of the early twentieth century. The 54,000-square-foot house, with its seventeenth- and eighteenth-century English antiques, is especially exciting during the Christmas holidays, when the historic house and garden are transformed into a winter wonderland. From the end of November and into the new year, the garden is aglow with lighting displays at every turn, and the house is brought to life with the sounds of merriment, lights, and themed holiday décor.

Detail from the foyer staircase.

— WOODSIDE, CALIFORNIA —

A beautifully decorated tree, large-scale wreath, and table set for light refreshments create a festive ambiance.

Above
In the dining room, antique hand-painted Venetian crystal stemware adds sparkle to each place setting.
Below
A lavishly decorated tree greets visitors in Filoli's elegant reception room. *Photography by Gino De Grandis, courtesy of Lui Photography*

The portrait in the study of Mrs. Roth was painted by Lloyd Sexton in 1981.

Midcentury Murano glass nativity figures adorn the coffee table in Filoli's Study. *Photography by Gino De Grandis, courtesy of Lui Photography*

In the dining room, the dining table and painting above the fireplace are original to the Bourn occupancy. Mrs. Roth's mother owned the china cupboard. The holiday dinner table and sideboard are decorated in a serene green-and-white color scheme.

 In another setting, the dining table is laden with sweet treats.

Little is known about how the Bourns, who built Filoli, celebrated Christmas. What we do know comes from the Roth family who bought the house after the Bourns died. In later years the extended Roth family would gather for large celebrations in the ballroom. Christmas trees would be decorated and placed throughout the house. The largest tree was in the reception room, often right in front of the foyer doors. Additional trees could be found in the family room/study and in the upstairs sitting room. Presents were always kept under the tree in the upstairs family room or sitting room. Mrs. Roth's daughter, Lurline Coonan, remembers that her mother would lock the door to keep the kids away from the piles of presents. On at least one occasion, the key was misplaced for a time and the grandchildren remember fears that presents would be delayed. Some presents did not fit beneath the tree. Perhaps one of the most memorable gifts were the ponies Mrs. Roth was known to give her grandchildren. The ponies would remain at Filoli for them to ride when they were visiting."

As for the décor, the house was filled with evergreens, candles, and fir trees, and leis from Hawaii welcomed visitors. Wreaths placed in every window were made from holly and evergreens grown at Filoli.

Today at Christmastime, visitors can enjoy the festively decorated house and magical outdoor light displays, where cozy fire pits and holiday libations beckon. Open daily for both daytime and evening admission, Holidays at Filoli offers a calming, welcome escape to beauty and nature at the end of each year.

ABOUT FILOLI. Filoli's beautiful name was coined by William Bowers Bourn II, owner of the Empire Mine, a thriving gold mine. He combined the first two letters of fight, love, live—key words in his credo, "To fight for a just cause, to love your fellowman, to live a good life." Built for his wife Agnes Moody Bourn, whom he married in 1881, the house was designed by San Francisco architect Willis Polk, who had already designed two other homes for the Bourns. But the married couple had a clear idea of the kind of house they wanted, based on the early eighteenth- to mid-nineteenth-century English country house. The eclectic result is a welcoming English Renaissance-inspired U-shaped building with relatively low hipped roofs and dormers. Classical elements include

 The 70-foot-long ballroom features five mural scenes that Ernest Peixotto painted of Muckross, a beloved Irish estate.

 Arching bare branches wrapped in white fairy lights create a magical arbor.

 In most grand houses, the staircase is part of the entry foyer. Not so at Filoli, where it is a dramatic surprise architectural element. Beautiful even in its undecorated state, at Holiday Traditions time, the black Belgian marble risers and wrought iron balustrade become the canvas upon which floral artists work their magic.

highest at 22 feet, 6 inches, followed by the reception room at 18 feet, 6 inches. Most major rooms were 17 feet high. In the fall of 1917, the Bourns moved into what William referred to as a home for Agnes. The house was not entirely finished at that time. The ballroom walls were simply painted white on white. It would be more than eight years before the addition of the five romantic murals with scenes based on views at Muckross, the Irish estate home of the Bourns' daughter Maud Vincent, which William loved but was no longer physically able to visit. The murals were painted and installed and the room was completed in 1926.

The gardens, planned with the help of artist and designer Bruce Porter, were created between 1917 and 1929 for Agnes, an avid gardener who founded a garden club. Following the Bourns' death, William P. Roth and his wife Lurline purchased the estate in 1937. Filoli was very much a family home for the Roths and their three children: Bill, Lurline, and Berenice.

During their residency, the Roths built a swimming pool, so beautifully designed and integral to the garden that it looked as though it had always been there. Mrs. Roth loved the garden and became involved in adding to its maple and magnolia trees, rhododendrons, roses, and other plants. Under her care, the Filoli garden became world famous, known for its exquisite horticultural collection. In 1973, Mrs. Roth was awarded the Distinguished Service Medal of the Garden Clubs of America. In 1975, the widowed Mrs. Roth gave the house, gardens and 125 acres of land to the National Trust for Historic Preservation. She gave the rest of the estate—529 acres—to Filoli Center. Today, it is a California State Historic Landmark and listed on the National Registry of Historic Places.

distinctive corner quoins, belt (or stream) courses, cornices, and French casement type windows. The imposing entrance portico is Italian baroque with handsome Tuscan columns. Brickwork is Flemish-bond. Spanish mission roof tiles add a California touch. On the exterior, brick cladding covers a steel superstructure. Interior walls are lath and plaster. While Polk designed the house, the Bourns would ultimately work with several architects, landscape designers, and other experts to achieve the overall vision of Filoli.

Work began on the house in 1914. At its completion, the house had fifty-six rooms, plus bathrooms and storerooms. Gracious interiors featured high ceilings. The ballroom was

 Large, lavishly decorated trees are a hallmark of a Filoli Holiday Traditions event. Designed to thrill, guaranteed to inspire, these trees feature well-thought-out themes and brilliant color schemes. Here, for endless enjoyment and instruction, is a gallery of Filoli Christmas trees.

 Tabletop trees recall "feather trees," a German invention introduced into the United States by German immigrants, who found them easy to pack for travel and useful year after year.

The 1749 Spanish Governor's Palace (originally the Presidio San Antonio Bejar) is one of the oldest houses in Texas. Some consider it San Antonio's most beautiful building. The double doors, carved in 1930 by Swiss woodcarver Peter Mansbendel, tell the story of Spanish exploration in the new world. The keystone shows the double-headed eagle, symbol of Spanish King Ferdinand VI (Hapsburg). Current palace shopping bags carry a more colorful crest. *Photography by architect David Strahan*

HOLIDAYS AT THE PRESIDIO
Spanish Governor's Palace

The elegant simplicity of the Spanish Governor's Palace seems a world away from the ornate Italianate, French second empire, Queen Anne, and other Victorian style homes on historic King William Street a mile or so away. The one-story, U-shaped structure surrounding a traditional Spanish courtyard is a design oasis. A visit to the Spanish Governor's Palace at Christmas is a gift of calm, a respite from exuberant Victorian excess.

— SAN ANTONIO, TEXAS —

What familiar Christmas decorations should one expect to see at the Spanish Governor's Palace during the holiday season? Only one—poinsettias. That elegant, red-velvet-leafed Mexican plant adds dramatic color to many rooms. It is thought that the plant was first associated with Christmas in sixteenth-century Mexico and that Franciscans decorated churches there with it for seventeenth-century Christmas events. The name poinsettia comes from Joel Roberts Poinsett, the first US ambassador to Mexico (1825–1829). In Mexico in 1828, Poinsett became enchanted by the brilliant red blooms (leaves) he saw there. He shipped some of the plants to his home in South Carolina and began propagating them. He sent them to friends and botanical gardens. The poinsettia quickly became widely popular. Now a traditional part of Christmas décor in interiors of all styles and periods, it seems especially fitting in this setting.

 In its stark simplicity, the interior seems almost modern, yet the ceiling reveals its venerable origins. The heavy *vigas* (load-bearing beams) and *jatillas* (smaller poles between the beams) would have been covered in twigs. Massed poinsettias, a Mexican plant brought to the United States by Joel Roberts Poinsett, the first US ambassador to Mexico, pay tribute to the season.

 The living room's massive stone floor was installed after San Antonio purchased the structure in 1929. The original flooring would have been compacted dirt or clay. The 1749 Captain's Office is visible at the far end, through an open door.

89

 The raised-hearth fireplace in the dining room is a
study in elegant simplicity with its tapered chimney
breast. Other fireplaces offer ingenious design
variety. One near the living room entry has a low
wall that directs heat into the room, preventing its
escape through the open door.

THE PALACE, now a National Historic Landmark, is a remnant of the Presidio San Antonio de Béjar (1722–1800s). It was built by the Spanish to protect the San Antonio de Valero Mission (The Alamo), nearby missions (that now make up the San Antonio Missions National Historical Park), and a growing Spanish colony. The date 1749—part of the design of the keystone above the front entrance—marks it as one of the oldest residential buildings in Texas. The carved, double-headed eagle from the coat-of-arms of Spanish King Ferdinand VI (of Hapsburg) marks it as a Spanish government building. Completed in 1749, the aristocratic eighteenth-century Spanish colonial town house was originally the *comandancia* (residence and working office) for the captain of the Presidio. When the capital of Spanish Texas moved from Los Adaes (east of Nacogdoches) to San Antonio, around 1772, the house became home to the captain, who also served as governor of the province.

 Recessed niches provide display space for important pottery and religious objects.

 A handsomely carved table, a polychrome statue of Madonna and child, and a small prayer stool offer a place for private worship.

The Presidio San Antonio Bejar (Bexar) declined in the early 1800s. In 1804, the last captain, José Menchaca, sold the six-room compound to Ignacio Pérez, governor of Texas from 1815 to 1817, and a former Spanish captain. By 1820, the Presidio was no longer a major military post. The nearby walled San Antonio de Valero Mission (Alamo) seemed protection enough for the area. A prominent merchant and land owner, Perez and his descendants remained in the house until the 1860s.

On June 4, 1836, Texas achieved its independence from Mexico, becoming the Republic of Texas and then the twenty-eighth state of the United States of America. Following the Civil War and changes in the neighborhood, the Perez family leased out their property. Reportedly, over the years it housed a bar, clothing store, produce store, tailor shop, pawn shop, and school.

In the late 1860s, E. Hermann Altgelt, founder of Comfort, a town in Kendall County, bought the house and lived there with his family at various times. His widow, Emma Murck Altgelt, owned the property until the early 1900s.

Eventually, the Spanish Governor's Palace fell into disrepair. In 1915, Adina Emilia De Zavala, who had moved from Houston to San Antonio to teach, pointed out that the building was important and should be preserved. This intrepid woman founded the De Zavala Chapter of the Daughters of the Republic of Texas in 1893. In 1912, she founded the Texas Historical and Landmarks Association.

A bedroom (*previous page*) contains a stylish baroque polychrome bed. At its foot, a trunk with a decorative interior provides storage. Near the window, a small table and chair serve as a writing desk.

 A floor brazier stood in for a fireplace.

De Zavala achieved her goal when the city of San Antonio purchased the Spanish Governor's Palace in 1928. Architect Harvey Partridge Smith, whose impressive credentials included study at Northwestern University, the University of Arizona, the Art Institute of Chicago, and Ecole des Beaux-Arts in Paris, was hired to supervise the restoration. He brought to bear expertise gained in his work with legendary architect Atlee Ayers and on the restoration and preservation of San Antonio missions. His preservation effort in 1929–30 saved as much of the original structure as possible. Spanish colonial furnishings were installed under his supervision, and in 1931, the building was opened as the Spanish Governor's Palace Museum.

 The education room was added in the late 1800s. Children's toys are on the table.

The spacious kitchen was a 1930 addition.

This beautifully glazed antique pottery jug is set near the entrance.

 The late 1800s education room opens onto the walled terrace, while the adjacent late 1700s dining room and the 1930s kitchen open into a passageway that leads to the terrace and courtyard beyond.

The expansive courtyard is a respite from the city. A massive gate opens to the historic heart of downtown.

A 12-foot Christmas tree in
Philadelphia Hall.

YULETIDE AT BAYOU BEND
Bayou Bend Collections and Gardens

Yuletide: Holiday Time at Bayou Bend is an annual tradition eagerly anticipated by thousands of Houstonians and takes place at the museum and former home of Houston's beloved philanthropist Ima Hogg. The festivities began more than twenty-five years ago with a desire to recall real and imagined holiday events, replete with period-appropriate decorations throughout the Bayou Bend house, according to museum director Bonnie Campbell.

Ima Hogg

Research soon revealed that while the tradition of holding celebratory parties was centuries old, holiday decorations did not become popular in America until the later decades of the nineteenth century. Yuletide celebrations focused a great deal on sharing sumptuous food and drink with family and friends. This discovery led to the pursuit of food history, period recipes, and table settings from the past.

It is impossible to re-create a party with empty plates. "One of Bayou Bend's docents, a professional artist, began to make *faux* food and drink for the installations," Campbell says. "Over the years, these mouth-watering creations have grown in number and variety, making Yuletide at Bayou Bend particularly unique."

Docents scour historical newspapers, diaries, and inventories and scrutinize paintings and engravings to create period-correct parties that also make the rooms sparkle. The elaborate, three-day installation process involves moving objects from storage, rearranging the house, and borrowing from private collections. Museum registrars, conservators, and preparations staff spend endless hours helping to inventory, handle, and protect the exhibition objects and interiors.

Finally, by the third Thursday of November, Yuletide at Bayou Bend opens. The docents and museum staff are exhausted. But they have once again given visitors a delightfully memorable present for the holiday season.

— HOUSTON, TEXAS —

Strolling Through American Holiday History
The festive stroll through decorated rooms is, in essence, a walk through 250 years of American holiday history.

The north façade is aglow with holiday lighting and decorated with wreaths and garlands. Stately portico columns are wrapped candy-cane fashion with red ribbon. *Photography by Bruce Bennett, courtesy Museum of Fine Arts, Houston*

PHILADELPHIA HALL, named for its rococo furnishings, features a grand sweeping staircase where a dazzling Christmas tree greets Yuletide visitors. "The tree is decorated with 7,000 lights and 3,500 ornaments," Campbell says. "The hallway is decorated to re-create idealized, romantic Christmases of old. It features the type of festive decorations and lavish greenery that, beginning in the 1930s, came to typify Yuletide celebrations at historic houses."

 The spacious drawing room adapts to a different
history-based scenario each yuletide (*right*). Above, the
dining table is set as though for a dinner hosted by
Benjamin Franklin. The card table is ready for a game of
Whist. *Photography by Bruce Bennett, courtesy Museum
of Fine Arts, Houston*

THE DRAWING ROOM (now called the formal living room) is the largest room at Bayou Bend. During most of the year, this room showcases a gallery of select furniture and portraits by three of America's distinguished early artists. But at yuletide it is transformed. One year it might be the setting for a Christmas dinner as hosted by Benjamin Franklin in 1775. "Celebrating his return from eleven years in London on behalf of the American colonies, the meal would be lavish. There would be a roasted boar's head and a large plum pudding," Campbell says.

Another year, the drawing room might features a card table scenario as shown in the photograph. "In the eighteenth century, card parties were a favorite form of entertainment during the holidays and year-round. They offered a rare opportunity for unmarried men and women to socialize," Campbell says. "In this setting, an exquisite eighteenth-century card table is set for a game of Whist. The white bone playing pieces are called 'fish' and are often carved in the shape of fish as seen here."

THE DINING ROOM. The glowing gold-leaf canvas wall covering was designed by New York artist William MacKay in 1927–28. It features hand-painted Texas dogwood branches and peonies, while field mice and butterflies add a touch of elegant whimsy. One yuletide, the dining table showed off a Thanksgiving dinner that might have been served in 1830 in Salem, Massachusetts. "It featured an elegant set of Chinese export porcelain of the kind often found in wealthy homes in New England," Campbell says. "Thanksgiving was the primary fall and winter holiday until the mid-1800s. There was no national annual Thanksgiving holiday until the Civil War, but the governors of New England states proclaimed state holidays annually after 1815. Thanksgiving was also the occasion for charitable giving of the type we associate with Christmas today." In that spirit, gifts for the poor are stashed in the pillowcases near the fireplace.

A sideboard is often the setting for a historical vignette. One year the display told the story of exotic Hawaiian anthuriums that Hogg received from Houston friends in the 1950s. Another year it was set with miniature buildings that created a sense of a small winter village.

 The dining room is the scene of an imagined 1830s Salem, Massachusetts, Thanksgiving dinner. Another scene features a chest-top display of a miniature holiday village. The box of exotic flowers recalls Christmas gifts Hogg received from neighbors. *Photography by Bruce Bennett, courtesy Museum of Fine Arts, Houston*

 Chillman Parlor recalls the 1863 holiday celebrations of a Texas family, showing shortages caused by the Civil War. Another year, the display told the story of a White House holiday snowball fight for Andrew Jackson's great nieces and nephews. Small tables eloquently depict holiday customs, and especially refreshments associated with a given place and period. *Photography by Bruce Bennett, courtesy Museum of Fine Arts, Houston*

THE CHILLMAN PARLOR and FOYER make up the Chillman Suite, named in honor of Dorothy Dawes Chillman. Mrs. Chillman, wife of James H. Chillman (the first director of the museum), was an interior decorator and close friend of Hogg's who helped develop Bayou Bend's period rooms. Ordinarily, furniture is in the Grecian style (1810–45) and the room is quite sedate. But during yuletide the parlor is transformed. "Here, the display reflects the memories of a Texas family and their Christmas in 1863," Campbell says. "Due to shortages caused by the Civil War, there are no candles because they were expensive. Decorations are handmade, including corn husk dolls and paper decorations cut from *Godey's Lady's Book*. Small packages are attached to the tree. The gifts that year were homemade, too. The area around the sofa looks in disarray—the mother had pulled up the carpet to make coats because Austin winters can be cold and no heavy fabric was available."

A tabletop display showed how a New York City hostess in the 1800s would have set out refreshments for gentlemen making a mad round of customary two-to-three-minute house calls.

One of the most humorous yuletide displays in Chillman Parlor portrays an 1835 party that Andrew Jackson held in the White House for his great-nieces and nephews and their guests. "The entertainment included dinner and games—even an indoor snowball fight," Campbell says. She cited research that recalled each child being given a few cotton snowballs (with a piece of candy inside) and invited to play snowball in the East Room, creating a scene of snow flurry.

THE MASSACHUSETTS ROOM'S dynamic blue walls, inspired by an eighteenth-century Portuguese chintz, are a dramatic backdrop for any period-inspired display. "The bedroom scene here imagines Anna Green Winslow, a twelve-year-old girl visiting 1770s Boston, as she is getting ready for an evening party. It is one of many social and holiday occasions she attended and mentioned in her diary," Campbell says. "Anna will dress in her most fashionable clothes and a stylish hairpiece, seen scattered around the room in true twelve-year-old style."

Another scene imagines Pope's Day, November 5, 1765, the English holiday known as Guy Fawkes' Day. "Until the 1760s, the day was marked by drinking, civil disorder, and the parading of effigies of hated figures of authority. Then, the Sons of Liberty persuaded leaders to turn the day into one of peaceful protest against the English king, tyranny, and injustice," Campbell says. "The event's wealthy sponsors have gathered at a punch party to celebrate their success. Relics of the day, including drums, conch shells, canes, and swords are scattered around the room. The red flag hanging over the fireplace is the Red Ensign, the British flag used in the colonies before the Revolution."

 Yuletide scenarios in the Massachusetts Room tell dramatically different stories—one of a young girl preparing for an exciting holiday party; the other of the gathering of celebrants of Pope's Day, their drums and swords at rest in the room. *Photography by Bruce Bennett, courtesy Museum of Fine Arts, Houston*

 A traditional eighteenth-century alcoholic punch for Pope's Day celebrants was most likely served in a large bowl, but may also have been served in a punch pot. *Photograph by Bruce Bennett, courtesy Museum of Fine Arts, Houston*

The vignette features a traditional eighteenth-century alcoholic punch served from a large bowl. "The punch pot [resembling an over-sized teapot] shows another popular way to serve punch," Campbell says. "This form was considered particularly well-suited to hot drinks, which would have been very welcome on a chilly November day in Boston."

 In the Massachusetts Room, a vignette displays a late-eighteenth-century dessert course. *Photograph by Bruce Bennett, courtesy Museum of Fine Arts, Houston*

THE BELTER PARLOR takes its name from cabinetmaker John Henry Belter, whose New York City factory made the furniture in this room. In the rococo revival style, this highly carved, ornate furniture was the most popular style in the mid-Victorian era. "The Christmas tree displayed here is decorated with homemade ornaments and gifts reflecting mid-Victorian customs for Christmas in America," Campbell says. At that time, she explains, gifts were not necessarily wrapped but simply set out for the children to see, and many were hung on the tree.

An 1850s family would celebrate Christmas gift-giving with a "spider-web" game. Each child is given a ribbon wrapped around furniture, draped over wall fittings, and tangled around lighting fixtures. He or she follows the ribbon until reaching a gift. For encouragement, small gifts and cornucopias filled with candy are attached to the ribbon along the way. "Although Christmas trees were becoming popular by the mid-1800s—notice the small table-top version in this room—they were by no means universal. Popular magazines like *St. Nicholas* described a variety of creative ways of presenting gifts," Campbell says.

 The Belter Parlor is named for the maker of the highly carved furniture most associated with the Victorian era. Naturally, the Christmas tree would be decorated in the Victorian style. A "spider-web" game of "find the gift at the end of the ribbon" seems very much at home in the exuberant parlor. *Photography by Bruce Bennett, courtesy Museum of Fine Arts, Houston*

THE MURPHY ROOM, named for Katharine Prentis Murphy, a close friend and fellow collector, contains a collection of late renaissance (1620–1690) and early baroque (1690–1730) furnishings. The striking black-and-white painted floor was inspired by late-seventeenth-century Boston portraits (probably containing painted floor cloths). One of the museum's most popular displays appeals to children of all ages and is called Toys for Good Little Girls and Boys, a history of toys and Christmas in America.

By the mid-1700s, when George Washington was buying gifts for his step-children, imported toys were available. But it was not until more than six decades later that Christmas became an occasion for gift-giving, and generations later that gift-wrapping became an art. The displays often show what gifts of toys would have looked like through the generations. "In 1969, the year of the moon landing, space and science fiction toys were popular," Campbell says. "Aluminum Christmas trees were a fashionable way to have a modern holiday."

 A yuletide visitor is likely to see a marvelous display of period accurate Christmas trees in the Murphy Room, with its handsome, heavily carved late Renaissance and early baroque furniture. Or, there might be a lavish exhibit of children's toys through decades. *Photography by Bruce Bennett, courtesy Museum of Fine Arts, Houston*

 Before Bayou Bend became a museum, the Pine Room was the library. Hogg covered walls with pine paneling inspired by mid-eighteenth-century paneling in a room at the Metropolitan Museum of Art in New York City. *Photography by Bruce Bennett, courtesy Museum of Fine Arts, Houston*

 Opposite page
Crowds gather early for the opening of Bayou Bend each yuletide. On Festive Family Fridays, giant puppets come out to play with younger guests. Museum staff oversee crafts tables and serve cocoa and hot apple cider. Children's choirs sing popular holiday songs. Yuletide Nights: Spirits of Holidays Past offers ages twenty-one and older nights of holiday cheer. Costumed actors bring the exhibition to life. Festive foods and drink adapted from historic recipes are served, and live music features favorite seasonal songs. *Photography by Kim Coffman, courtesy Museum of Fine Arts, Houston*

Ima Hogg used Bayou Bend's PINE ROOM as the library. A yuletide setting features Windsor chairs, reading lamps, and a nineteenth-century hooked rug. They provide a cozy atmosphere for reading, card playing, or conversation. "The mantel, decorated for the Christmas season, serves to remind visitors of happy memories they have spent warming up by a fire on a cold winter's evening," says Campbell.

Bayou Bend's exterior is adorned with lights, garlands, and wreaths, and the massive portico columns are wrapped candy-cane fashion with wide red ribbon. The former home presents a host of holiday events featuring seasonal music, food, and activities. Yuletide Nights: Spirits of Holidays Past offers those ages twenty-one and older a spirited night of holiday cheer. Costumed re-enactors bring the exhibition to life, festive foods and drinks adapted from historical recipes are served, and live music features seasonal favorites. Festive Family Fridays are early evenings targeted to children but enjoyed by all ages. Life-sized puppets—a snowman, gingerbread man, and Father Christmas, to name a few—visit with the guests, while the staff oversee crafts tables and serve cocoa and hot apple cider. Holiday Family Days offer free afternoon activities, along with holiday songs and refreshments. The River Oaks Chamber Orchestra presents a Yuletide Coffee and Concert under a magical party tent perched off Bayou Bend's Diana Terrace; 120 guests at each seating are captivated by the brass quintet while sipping a variety of holiday cheer.

 The Shop at Bayou Bend is a treasure trove of holiday gifts. Museum director Bonnie Campbell says these items reflect the quality, craftsmanship, and beauty of the collection and gardens. *Photography courtesy Museum of Fine Arts, Houston*

THE SHOP at Bayou Bend is a treasure trove of holiday-related items and unique gifts. Shoppers discover carefully chosen items that reflect the quality, craftsmanship, and beauty of the collection and gardens. Many items are made exclusively for Bayou Bend, including custom ties, scarves, jewelry, pottery, candles, teas, and one-of-a-kind wood bowls and vases made from trees that have fallen on the property.

CELEBRATING *the* HOLIDAYS *with* IMA HOGG

Bonnie Campbell and her staff offer a glimpse into how Ima Hogg celebrated the holidays, as gleaned from "Reminiscences of Life in the Texas Governor's Mansion," Ima Hogg Paper, Briscoe Center for American History, Austin, Texas.

Hogg believed Christmas was for families. As a child growing up in Texas, young Ima and her three brothers—Will, Mike, and Tom—exchanged small gifts on Christmas Day. Gifts were usually books they had inscribed with their names and a message or mementos they had made under their mother's direction. Later, the family celebrated at home with carols, music, and dinner. On New Year's Day, the Hoggs welcomed friends to their home. They continued this tradition when they moved into the Texas Governor's Mansion in 1891. Years later, Hogg recalled her mother's beautiful New Year's Day receptions. She described the linens, the catered delicacies, and the floral centerpieces that adorned the tables. She recalled the smilax and holly her mother draped around the windows and the mistletoe peeping from the gaslight chandeliers. And she remembered the music and dancing. During her years at Bayou Bend (1928–1965), Hogg replicated some of her mother's customs.

Some years, Christmas Day at Bayou Bend was low-key. She would open gifts with her housekeeper and chauffeur, whom she considered family. This was true especially after she lost her brothers (Will in 1930, Mike in 1941, and Tom in 1949). In the 1940s and '50s, Hogg often invited a few cousins for Christmas Day luncheon. Six to eight guests, sometimes quite young members of her extended family, would enjoy a superbly cooked meal beautifully presented on one of Hogg's ceramic collections.

Hogg also welcomed her friends during the season. She decorated with holly and pine cone garlands on the staircases and over the fireplace in the Pine Room. She arranged white flowers, berries, yaupon, and other foliage from her garden in ceramic bowls. She placed white poinsettias in Philadelphia Hall and the Drawing Room. She placed pine cones on the fireplace logs in the Drawing Room. She told a journalist that she particularly loved her memories of the Pine Room because that was where she had celebrated Christmas. She described eggnog parties there on Christmas Day, and friends remember card parties in that room. Occasionally, she invited parties of thirty or more for a holiday dinner. For these, she set up small tables in the Pine Room and Massachusetts Room and decorated them with bowls of white flowers. She also explained that in the 1930s her brother Mike and his wife Alice, who lived next door, hosted a reception on Christmas Day.

Whether Hogg was at home or traveling during the Christmas season, she always remembered her friends with cards and small gifts. For years her card featured an image of Bayou Bend drawn by Texas artist Buck Schiwetz. One year she reproduced a Picasso mother and child and included a recipe for a "Bayou Bend Cocktail." Another year, she sent special friends a book that explained how to appreciate and understand classical music.

Windows in the Pine Room bay reflect the sparkling Christmas tree lights. Hogg traditionally placed a tree there. *Photograph by Bruce Bennett, courtesy Museum of Fine Arts, Houston*

IMA HOGG
and BAYOU BEND

Portrait of Ima Hogg, 1971, by Robert C. Joy; Museum of Fine Arts, Houston, the Bayou Bend Collection, gift of Ima Hogg. *Photograph by Thomas R. DuBrock, courtesy Museum of Fine Arts, Houston*

IMA HOGG was born in the small town of Mineola, Texas, in 1882, named after the heroine of an epic poem written by her uncle. Her father, businessman James Stephen Hogg, became the first native-born governor of Texas in 1891 and the family moved to Austin. These formative years living in the Governor's Mansion established Hogg's lifelong interest in politics, history, and American antiques. She recalled later the thrill of sleeping in the bed that had belonged to Sam Houston, one of the most celebrated political figures in Texas. Her family also influenced her interests. From her father she acquired an abiding love of Texas, a sense of public duty, a fascination with history, and affection for flowers and trees. From her mother she inherited a talent for music, a love of beauty, and a discerning eye that recognized good taste.

Despite many important civic contributions—the Houston Symphony; the Museum of Fine Arts, Houston; mental health; public education; and historic preservation—Hogg is best known for assembling a remarkable collection of Americana, one of the finest in the country. Bayou Bend is a decorative arts scholar's paradise. Approximately 2,500 objects in twenty-eight room settings and galleries reflect American decorative arts styles from 1620 to 1876. This astounding collection began with the purchase of an American Queen Anne armchair similar to one she had seen in an artist's studio while sitting for her portrait in 1920. (Many years later, she purchased the very chair that she had seen.) Museum records quote her as saying, "From the time I acquired my first Queen Anne armchair in 1920, I had an unaccountable compulsion to make an American collection for some Texas museum." By the early 1950s, the purchases had increased in scope and quantity. During this decade she acquired many of the collection's finest eighteenth-century colonial American furniture and paintings.

In the 1920s, Will Hogg and his brother Mike helped develop River Oaks, a planned garden community west of downtown Houston. They selected 14 acres for a residence to share with their sister, Ima. The site was, according to Hogg, "nothing but a dense thicket." Nestled in the curve of Buffalo Bayou (hence the name Bayou Bend) and covered by undergrowth and tall trees, this rugged acreage was a far cry from the extraordinary gardens she subsequently created.

The mansion is surrounded by formal gardens and lush bayou woodlands. Hogg developed the landscape with passion and dedication over more than four decades. A southern influence is evident throughout; a dazzling variety of azalea and camellia bushes graces the property, along with flowering trees such as magnolia, crepe myrtle, and dogwood. The formal gardens are a rare surviving example of American landscape design popular during the country estate era (1890–1940); these landscapes feature garden "rooms" that seem to extend from the house, water features as focal points, and classical statuary. A sense of proportion, harmony, and restraint is everywhere. Bayou Bend is recognized as the first historic public garden in Texas to practice organic gardening.

The home was one of the first to be built in River Oaks, now one of Houston's most beautiful and prestigious neighborhoods. Hogg worked closely with Houston architect John F. Staub on a design that incorporates elements of several styles. Massing is neo-Palladian (a central block flanked by wings), imposing columns recall the plantations of the American South, and light pink stucco cladding and decorative cast iron reflect the Spanish Creole influence of New Orleans. Hogg dubbed the eclectic style "Latin Colonial" and deemed it appropriate for Houston.

To provide suitable settings for the extraordinary antiques that Hogg had begun collecting in 1920, Staub designed simple but stately interiors based on classic eighteenth- and early nineteenth-century architectural traditions. In Hogg's bedroom and sitting room, he installed floorboards and paneling from two eighteenth-century houses in Massachusetts. The two-story, twenty-four-room house was completed in 1928. While Mike married and moved out in 1929, and Will died in 1930, Ima continued to live there until 1965.

In 1957, Ima Hogg donated Bayou Bend and her collection to the Museum of Fine Arts, Houston. She continued to live in her home while she oversaw its transformation into a museum, and in 1966, she presided over its opening. In the museum magazine, *Inside/Out*, Fall/Winter 2014/2015, Campbell quotes Ima Hogg: "I hope in a modest way Bayou Bend may serve as a bridge to bring us closer to the heart of an American heritage which unites us."

The altered façade of the Conde-Charlotte house features Greek revival Doric columns on the lower level and Corinthian columns on the upper level. Flags of the five nations that once ruled the area fly above the entry. *Photography by Chad Riley, courtesy Chad Riley Photography/ Mobile, Alabama and Conde-Charlotte Museum*

CHRISTMAS IN STYLE
Condé-Charlotte Museum

Condé-Charlotte is the name given to the house built by banker Jonathan Kirkbride on the site of the military fortification, which began life in 1711 as Ft. Louis de la Louisiane in honor of the French king Louis XIV. In 1720 it became Ft. Condé, named for a French officer. In 1763, the English acquired the fort and renamed it Ft. Charlotte (honoring the wife of King George III). After American troops captured the city in 1813 it grew, and the fort was no longer needed. Mr. Kirkbride purchased the property and built a house for his family.

In 1940, the Historic Mobile Preservation Society purchased the Kirkbride house and began restoration. The 2-foot-thick brick floors and the outlines of four 6-by-8-foot jail cells were discovered in the main house (they are visible now through a glass-covered hole in the parlor floor).

The National Society of the Colonial Dames of America in the State of Alabama purchased the house in 1957 and completed the restoration. For a while it was used as an office for supervisors of the twin tunnels being built beneath the Mobile River. In 1974, the Condé-Charlotte house, newly refurbished, opened as a museum.

To visit at Christmastime is to revel in a house of many styles. Originally federal style, this gracious residence later took on the new, more popular Greek Revival style, boasting Doric brick columns on the first level of the two-story entry portico, and Corinthian wood columns on the second level.

Interior furnishings reflect the house's varied history. Many of the rooms are given styles associated with the nation that controlled the fort during a particular time period—a delight for those who study period furnishings. This includes the French (1709–1763), British (1763–1780), Spanish (1780–1812), American (1813–1861), and Confederate (1861–1865).

— MOBILE, ALABAMA —

 Large, open doorways provide sweeping views of second-floor bedrooms; each features a furniture style representing one of the five nations whose flags fly above the entry.

 A Christmas tree graces the parlor, outfitted with Confederate-era rococo furniture, the most popular Victorian-period style.

 Period-appropriate rooms show furnishings styles of particular eras. The Confederate double parlors are handsomely furnished in rococo pieces, the most popular Victorian-era style.

 This bedroom contains a handsome secretary and beautifully designed cradle. An intricately designed rug adds color.

 Gift packages artfully wrapped by Christine Warren and handcrafted ornaments trim the beautiful parlor tree.

1711. The first fort on the site was a stockade built by the French. They called it Ft. Louis de la Louisiane (in honor of King Louis XIV).

1720. The fort became Ft. Condé in honor of French military leader Henri Condé.

1724. Within the stockade, the French built a permanent brick fort, completed in 1735. (A reconstruction from French archive drawings stands on the site today.)

1763. England acquired the fort at the end of the Seven Years War, renaming it Ft. Charlotte (for the wife of King George III). Major Farmar was commandant.

1780. Spain seized the fort and the city of Mobile.

1813. President Madison ordered American troops to capture Mobile (ending Spain's aid of the British). The city grew. No fort was needed.

1820. Congress declared the fort surplus and it was sold at auction. The fort was demolished, and the site parceled as lots and sold.

1822. The city of Mobile bought two lots on the south side of the fort on which to build a jail, which was completed in 1824. It was used until about 1840, according to records.

1849. Jonathan Kirkbride, who had come to Mobile as a child from Mt. Holly, New Jersey, bought the property, built a house, and moved in with his wife and family. Kirkbride established himself as a banker, owner of a hardware business, and master builder. The property remained in the Kirkbride family until 1926.

1940. The Historic Mobile Preservation Society purchased the house and began restoration. The 2-foot-thick brick floors and the outlines of four 6-by-8-foot jail cells were discovered in the main house. During World War II, the house was loaned to the US Navy for use as an officer's club.

1957. The National Society of the Colonial Dames of America in the State of Alabama purchased the house and completed restoration. It temporarily became the supervision office for the construction of twin tunnels beneath the Mobile River.

1974. The Condé-Charlotte house, newly refurbished, opened to the public as a museum.

 Notable furniture in the American dining room includes the Sheraton drop-leaf mahogany dining table. Above the mantel hangs a classic federal-style mirror.

 Swags of greenery decorate the façade of the Condé-Charlotte house, which features Greek Revival Doric columns on the lower level and Corinthian columns on the upper level. *Photography by Chad Riley, courtesy of Chad Riley Photography / Mobile, Alabama, and Condé-Charlotte Museum*

 The French Empire–style furniture in a sitting room and bedroom belonged to the Batré family, who were descended from early settlers in the area.

FRENCH. The French Sitting Room is furnished as it would have been during the Second Restoration of Bourbon (1815–1830). Key pieces include an Empire chest, Louis Philippe table, Empire *bergères*, and a Napoleonic desk. A unique accessory is a highly decorative guitar inlaid with mother-of-pearl. The guitar was said to have belonged to Jerome Bonaparte, who brought it from France when he married Betty Paterson of Baltimore in 1803. This room is a treasure trove of object d'art. The adjoining French Bedroom reflects the Charles X period (1824–1830). The French Empire rosewood furniture belonged to the Batré family, descendants of early settlers in the area. A Charles X *trumeau* mirror features reverse painting on glass above the mirror. Numerous small objects enliven this room. On the floor is a prized Aubusson rug.

ENGLISH. The English Room is decorated with Major Farmar, commandant of Fort Charlotte in 1763, in mind. A portrait of George III hangs above the mantel, and there is an engraving of Queen Charlotte and the Prince Royal. The famous English furniture maker Chippendale is well represented in pieces featuring his innovative design motifs: a sofa with classically simple Marlborough legs, a pie-crust table, a Chinese Chippendale pier table, and a side chair with ball-and-claw feet.

The English were masters at mixing furniture from around the globe. True to that trait, the English Room contains many items of Dutch origin. Among these are brass candlesticks, two-branch candelabra, and several Delft vases. Other noted objects include a Queen Anne mirror, Battersea enamel miniature of Major Farmar, Wedgwood featheredge cachepots, and a George III silver tankard by John Senzilon of London.

AMERICAN. It's not surprising that the furniture in the American Dining Room (1813–1825 time period) features some British pieces: a Sheraton drop-leaf mahogany dining table (ca. 1810) and two Hepplewhite tables (ca. 1790). However, the Hepplewhite-style corner cupboard is a North Carolina piece, ca. 1810. The banjo clock is by Aaron Willard of Boston, and the silver is also American. The silver tea-and-coffee service is by Simon Chaudron of Philadelphia and Mobile; he was a Frenchman who settled in the Vine & Olive Colony, now Demopolis, Alabama. A silver ladle is by Johnson and Reat, Baltimore and Richmond silversmiths. I. David made the six serving spoons; sugar tongs are by W. Rae; and Conning, a Mobile silversmith, made six spoons. The cut-glass punch bowl is Pittsburgh, ca. 1820.

THE CONFEDERATE. Double parlors represent the period 1850–1860, when the Confederate flag flew over the South. Rosewood and mahogany Victorian furniture fills both parlors. The what-not stand, a response to the Victorian love of small objects, fills one corner of the room, its elaborate Gothic scrollwork transforming a utilitarian piece of furniture into a fascinating sculptural object. The rosewood card table tells a story of newfound leisure time. The papier-mâché, round, tilt-top table with mother-of-pearl inlays is an example of the Victorian love of surface embellishment. Mobile, Alabama, artist P. Homer created the portrait of James Howard Macy that hangs in the parlor. There are daguerreotypes and a host of intriguing decorative objects in these two parlors.

SPANISH. The Spanish influence—missing in the interior—is seen in the beautiful Spanish Garden. Inspired by old plans and records, it is typical of a late-eighteenth-to-early-nineteenth-century garden in Spain. The courtyard well is built of handmade radial bricks excavated for the tunnels beneath the Mobile River. Walkways are made of flagstone, reminiscent of early paths made from recycled flagstone used as ballast on sailing ships. Ornamental fountain tiles replicate old Spanish tiles. Plants include imported (azaleas from France) and native species.

The replicated fort is the anchor for Fort Condé Village, with its brick streets and gas streetlamps, to which period-appropriate buildings are being moved. The fort and village are fitting backdrops for the Condé-Charlotte Museum, which is still owned and operated by the National Society of the Colonial Dames of America in the State of Alabama. The house, listed on the National Register of Historic Places and open year-round, is especially enchanting during the holiday season, when all of Mobile is alive with the sights, sounds, and aromas of Christmas.

The bed in the French empire-style bedroom is arranged campaign fashion—snugly parallel to the wall, which frees up floor space. The furniture belonged to the Batré family descended from early area settlers. The rug is an Aubusson.

The kitchen's brick floor is a reminder that this home was built on the foundation of an old jail.

 Above the mantel in the British-style bedroom is a portrait of England's King George III.

 A wreath adorns the west gate during the Christmas season.

Salisbury House is basically a Tudor manor house. Gothic-style porches and a brick Carolean-style section give the impression of changes and alterations over time. The Weeks were inspired by the King's House in Salisbury, England.

A HOLLY AND IVY HOLIDAY
Salisbury House

For more than eighteen years, Salisbury House has hosted the Holly & Ivy holiday tour. This event showcases some of the most notable historic homes in Des Moines, including Terrace Hill (the Governor's Mansion), Hoyt Sherman Place, the Rollins Mansion, the Chamberlain Estate, and private homes in the historic South of Grand neighborhood. At Salisbury House, rooms are individually decorated by local florists, home furnishing stores, and interior decorators so that guests can expect something entirely different each year, according to Katie Wengert, Salisbury House Foundation.

Of course, any time of the year is a good time to visit this fascinating structure, which combines a Tudor manor with Gothic porches and a brick Carolean-style addition. In 1921, cosmetic magnate Carl Weeks and his wife, Edith Van Slyke Weeks, saw the inspiration for the dream home they planned to build—the fifteenth-century King's House in Salisbury, England. Famously quoted as saying, "If you can dream it, you can build it," Weeks did just that.

— DES MOINES, IOWA —

 Two antique classical columns frame a romantic winter view of Salisbury House, built by cosmetics king Carl Weeks and his wife Edith. *Photography courtesy Salisbury House*

 Salibury House and gardens are lovingly decorated for the annual Holly & Ivy holiday tour.

Des Moines architects Boyd & Moore collaborated with architect William Whitney Rasmussen of New York on the design of Salisbury House for Carl and Edith. Construction began in 1923 on the house and a caretaker's cottage on an 11-acre plot on Tonawanda Drive. Modern handmade tiles covered some of the roof, but seventeenth-century tiles from Trafalgar Park, Lord Nelson's estate in England, were also incorporated. Other English imports included exterior lead gutters and downspouts, knapped flint stones, sixteenth-century oak ceiling beams, paneling and flooring, and numerous antique fireplaces.

 The house's surprising textures and unusual window composition enrich and enliven a subdued landscape.

Opposite page/Clockwise from top
At the main entry, twin urns hold decorated lanterns. *Photograph by Kerri Hayes*

The massive door holds a large Christmas wreath. *Photograph by Peg Hammer*

The slightly ajar door offers a peek at the inviting interior. *Photograph by Kerri Hayes*

 The north entry offers a clear view through the house.

 A grand tree decorates the Great Hall with its beautiful minstrel loft and heavily timbered ceiling. *Photograph by Kerri Hayes*

Children's toys surround the base of the tree—unwrapped, as they would have been before gift-wrapping became popular. *Photograph by Kerri Hayes*

While the patina of old-money, Old World was important to Carl and Edith Weeks, they were typical New World comfort-loving Americans. Practical considerations included an elevator to serve the four floors. Coal-fired steam radiators ensured winter warmth. A central light control switch, dishwasher, gas dryer, and sophisticated telephone system added convenience and efficiency.

Financing such a massive structure is always a concern, even to millionaires. When real costs began to exceed estimates, it is said that architect Rasmussen proved himself a master of creative financing. He suggested that Carl Weeks' cosmetics business, Armand Co., underwrite a portion of the mansion's construction cost. Easlier, Rasmussen had suggested that Weeks publicize his home building project in the company's folksy newsletter, resulting in an onslaught of donated items. The financial move was the first of several that ensured that the Weeks family would continue to occupy Salisbury House through economic ups and downs until 1954.

The Weeks moved into their new home in 1926. In 1928 the 22,500-square-foot, four-story mansion was completed at a cost of $1.5 million. It contained forty-two rooms, including seventeen bedrooms and sixteen bathrooms. There was adequate space for Carl, Edith, and their four sons: Charles, William, Evert (Hud), and Lafayette (Lafe).

 All-red ornaments on the tree bring rich color into the library. At night, lights from the tree and a standing lamp cast a romantic glow reflected in the glass doors of library shelves, which hold 3,000 books, many of them rare and first edition.

Another $1.5 million was spent for thousands of collectibles and furnishings including antique decorative arts, tapestries, fine art, and rare books.

THE LIBRARY at Salisbury House is a treasure trove of 3,500 rare and first-edition books, including hand-illuminated thirteenth-century psalteries. Among the sixty Bibles is a leaf from the original printing of the Gutenberg Bible. There is an eighteen-century Qu'ran and a first edition Book of Mormon. Signed documents and books by Abraham Lincoln, Ernest Hemingway, James Joyce, Charles Dickens, Queen Elizabeth I, Joseph Smith, and D. H. Lawrence line the shelves.

Art works by Anthony Van Dyck, Sir Lawrence Alma-Tadema, Sir Thomas Lawrence, Joseph Stella, Lillian Genth, Jean Despujol, George Romney, Eduard Charlemont, John Carroll, and Leon Kroll adorn the walls. During the 1920s, the Weeks' support boosted Stella's career; they commissioned two works— *Apotheosis of the Rose* and *The Birth of Venus*. These internationally acclaimed works remain in the Salisbury House collection.

In the Commons Room hangs a magnificent portrait of Cardinal Dominico Rivarola, ca. 1600s.
Photograph by Peg Hammer

 Carl and Edith Weeks championed artists, including Joseph Stella, whose *Apotheosis of the Rose* hangs in the breakfast room.

 Opposite
The Commons Room chimney breast is heavily carved. Overhead is a Gothic tracery ceiling.

In 1954, Iowa State Education Association (ISEA) purchased the home and used it as headquarters until 1998. Salisbury House was added to the National Register of Historic Places in 1977. The Salisbury House Foundation purchased the house, grounds (9.4 acres), and collections in the late 1990s and converted the site into a museum. A special exhibit offers family photographs and newspaper clippings. In the boys' wing of the house are forty interpretive panels that depict the life and times of the Weeks family during their residency. The house is on the List of Registered Historic Places in Iowa.

Sconces and other surfaces in the Commons
Room are decorated for the holidays.
Photographs by Kerri Hayes

Holiday Greetings from

the three bachelors at

Salisbury House

Carl, William & Lafe Weeks

Through the Years
COSMETICS KING CARL WEEKS and SALISBURY

1876. Carl Weeks is born in Linn County, Iowa, to Charles and Laura Chamberlain Weeks

1889. Thirteen-year-old Carl Weeks moves to Des Moines, works in his maternal uncle's drug store, and later enrolls at Highland Park College to study pharmacy.

1892. Carl graduates from college.

1902. Carl Weeks and brother Leo join D. Weeks drug company, founded by his mother's family, the Chamberlains, and their brother Deyet. (The company manufactures over-the-counter medications and face powder.)

1907. Carl Weeks marries Edith Van Slyke.

1908. Carl and Leo Weeks take over the company after Deyet's death and found the D. C. Leo Company. (Carl creates a combination of cold cream and face powder, which becomes makeup foundation—the core of Carl's business success.

1915. Carl Weeks forms the Armand Company, marketing its product line across the United States, Canada, Mexico, Australia, France, and England.

1923. Carl and Edith Weeks build Salisbury house and move into it in 1926.

1934. The Weeks family deeds Salisbury House to Drake University, with the proviso that the Weeks continue to occupy it until 1954.

1950. Following World War II, competition from Revlon and other cosmetics companies constricts Armand Company growth. Carl merges the company with Weeks & Leo Company, retiring at age seventy-seven.

Greetings from Salisbury House And best wishes for a Merry Christmas and a Happy New Year.
Carl & Edith Weeks

 Vintage Christmas cards recall the happy holidays that the Weeks celebrated at Salisbury House.

Greetings from Salisbury House And best wishes for a Merry Christmas and a Happy New Year.
Carl & Edith Weeks

1954. Drake and the Weeks family broker a deal with the Iowa State Education Association (ISEA), who purchase the property and collections for around $200,000. The ISEA maintains its headquarters at Salisbury House for forty-five years.

1955. Edith Weeks dies.

1962. Carl Weeks dies.

1999. The estate is purchased by the newly formed Salisbury House Foundation, whose mission is to preserve, interpret, and share the international significance of Salisbury House and its collections as a historic house museum for the educational and cultural benefit of the public.

From the top of the tower at East Terrace, an Italianate Villa on the Brazos River, owner J. W. Mann could see boatloads of brick from his factory en route to distant destinations. *Photography by architect David Strahan*

TERRACES ON THE BRAZOS
East Terrace

East Terrace, a handsome house in the Italianate Villa style (commonly called the Hudson River style because it was so popular there) was originally terraced down to the edge of the Brazos River in Waco, Texas. Today, a street intervenes. But when J. W. Mann and his Poughkeepsie, New York-born wife, Cemira Twaddle Mann, bought the house and added on to it, Mann could watch boatloads of brick made in his factory float past by either strolling down the terraces to water's edge or from a high floor in the tower cupola. The brick's distinctive pink color, created by Brazos River sand, gives the house its soft, welcoming color and is at home in the Texas landscape. The asymmetrical silhouette is both elegant and romantic.

When the Manns and their sons, Howard and J. W. Jr., moved into the house, the ground floor consisted of an entrance hall, a home office for J. W., the family sitting room, and a small parlor. On the second floor were three bedrooms and a hall with a stair to the cupola. The kitchen was detached, a safety measure in an era in which kitchen fires were feared.

In 1880, six years after the family moved in, they added the large dining room that connects to the kitchen. The space above the dining room was made into a large dormitory-style bedroom. The 1873 Texas or entertainment wing—at right angles to the original house—contains two floors of large rooms—reception parlors on the ground floor, grand ballroom on the second. This wing surely reflects the family's growing wealth and importance in the community.

— WACO, TEXAS —

The entry hall offers a view into the original sitting room of the twice remodeled and enlarged structure. The chandelier once hung in the home of Governor Pat M. Neff.

The ground floor houses two parlors that can be separated by huge sliding doors. Today, the first parlor, named in honor of Dorothy Callan, is furnished with a collection of Victorian furnishings, a gift from the Callan estate. The second parlor's "suite" of carved rosewood furniture is a gift from the estate of Marcellus S. Brooks Sr. The double parlors have twin fireplaces for chilly winter days and evenings. Rows of floor-to-ceiling windows fitted with light and heat-controlling shutters create a sense of elegance and result in cool and pleasant spaces for entertaining even in Texas summers in an era before air-conditioning.

The new wing had its own entrance, making it easy for as many as fifty couples in full evening dress and horse-drawn carriages to arrive in style. They could step into the double reception parlors or ascend a handsome staircase to the dazzling second-floor ballroom. Running the full length of the wing, and with its high ceiling, the grand ballroom is grand indeed. Rhythmic rows of floor-length windows were (and are) both elegant and practical. They made this room literally the coolest ballroom in Waco—an important factor for summertime balls at East Terrace. Beautiful fireplaces added warmth and dancing flames for cooler weather.

 Small holiday decorations
brighten a bedroom.

It's not a stretch to imagine that East Terrace was the scene of enthusiastic Christmas celebrations, including balls. "Mrs. Mann was a charter member of the Central Christian Church. Because of this, it can be assumed that Christmas services were probably a key part of celebrating the season," says Stephanie Martinez, display coordinator for East Terrace.

Mann's home office, to the right of the entry, houses a glass-door barrister's bookcase containing encyclopedia, gifts to his son. Above the mantel is a portrait of Mann as director of the Waco Bank.

Previous page
An oil portrait of early Waco Judge Toland hangs above the mantel. On the hearth is a statue, *Niabi and Daughter*, which belonged to the Mann family.

 Above the Hepplewhite banquet table in the dining room, added in 1800, hangs a crystal chandelier, gift of Roger and Lacy Rose Conger. The table is set with festive china from the family's collection, which included Haviland porcelain made in Limoges, France. Windows in this elegant room are dressed with shutters and curtains (today called draperies) topped by a distinctive swag-and-jabot design.

A HOLIDAY TOUR. At the river-front entrance, double doors open into a gracious entry hall. To one side is J. W.'s home office. His portrait hangs over the mantel. From this small room, he conducted much of his business, civic, and social affairs. His company's kilns supplied brick for many Waco homes, public buildings, and Waco's Suspension Bridge (which required 2,700,000 bricks). With his brother, Thomas Mann, J. W. (nicknamed Sallie) dealt in real estate and other businesses. He was a director of the Waco Building and Loan Association. From 1884–1892, he was president of the Waco National Bank (which became the First National Bank of Central Texas). His civic duties included serving as an alderman representing Waco's Fifth Ward. J. W. did not have a formal education, but valuing it, he gave his son Howard a set of encyclopedias—expensive books in those days. They still reside in a barrister's glass-door bookcase in the home office.

THE SITTING ROOM. This room is original to the house and furnished with pieces that belonged to Cemira Mann: a small Victorian desk, a pair of French porcelain vases, two bamboo-turned side chairs, a platform rocker, and a statue entitled *Niabi and Daughter*. The chandelier, which originally hung in the Austin Avenue home of Governor Pat M. Neff, was a gift to East Terrace by Governor Neff's daughter, Hallie Maude Neff Wilcox.

THE DINING ROOM. The Manns appreciated gracious space, and the 1880 dining room addition reflects that. Martinez says that the dining room was probably the scene of festive holiday meals. "They probably had quite a spread laid out in their dining room," she says. "The table and room had plenty of space for visitors."

Furnishing historic houses is often a challenge, but the East Terrace had its champions. Roger and Lacy Rose Conger gave the crystal chandelier made in Czechoslovakia, as a memorial to their son following his death. He had planned to use it in his own home. The mahogany Hepplewhite-style banquet-size dining table was a gift from the Williams family in memory of C. B. Williams. Dr. John Burgess's gifted his own painting of a South Fourth Street house that was subsequently demolished.

The dining room's Haviland Limoges porcelain belonged to the Mann family. A distinctive dinnerware and giftware made of the fine white kaolin clay of Limoges, France, it is elegantly thin, translucent, very strong, legendary, and much copied.

 The kitchen, originally detached from the main house, was connected during the 1800 remodeling that added the spacious dining room.

 The third and last remodeling added an entertainment wing, called the Texas Wing, with its own entry. On the ground floor are double parlors. Furniture is mainly hand-carved mahogany. Many items are from a collection by Dorothy Callan, a gift from her estate. The second parlor contains carved rosewood furniture from the Marcellus S. Brooks Sr. estate. The rug in this room is a Bartiari made in Iran.

A second-floor grand ballroom is decorated with fantasy figures.

A Christmas tree holds forth on the landing, while the staircase leading to the cupola is treated to garlands and ribbon.

 Candy-covered objects make a dandy
centerpiece. They were made by local designers,
who are invited to contribute nonperiod
decorations throughout the house.

 The walnut canopy bed in the nursery was a gift from the Woody Callan Jr. collection. A hooked rug warms the floor.

 The Texas Wing hallway holds a nativity scene and a baroque angel.

THE DORMITORY BEDROOM. Located on the second floor above the dining room, it had as many as six beds—for guests who came for parties and stayed! Visitors today see a Victorian walnut bed and dresser (gift of the Compton family) which in its day might have been seen in a Sears, Roebuck Catalog for about $67.

THE MASTER BEDROOM. A modest-sized space, it is furnished with an antique walnut bed original to the house.

There are many areas and items of interest to explore in this splendid, convivial house. Visitors walk through this beautifully restored home year-round, but the most thrilling time for a visit is Christmastime—truly the most magical time of the year.

Garden staff and volunteers make
the wreaths and roping.

A JINGLE BELLE CHRISTMAS
Oatlands Historic House and Garden

The mansion at Oatlands Historic House and Garden inspires romantic visions of leisurely house tours, gracious teas, candlelight strolls, and truly magical Christmas décor. All of these visions are realized every holiday season. Additionally, there are shows, art exhibits, shopping, caroling, a gingerbread house contest, and special historic displays and exhibits. Oatlands is a lively holiday house with a great deal to do and see.

Fashions from select time periods during the history of Oatlands made a statement one Christmas with displays of women's clothing. Although none were from the Carter or Eustis families who lived at Oatlands, these garments visually told stories of some of the women who had lived in the mansion during the past two centuries. They gave visitors a sense of what life was like for the Oatlands women who had worn them. It's likely that this powerful display will be revisited in the future.

— LEESBURG, VIRGINIA —

 George Carter's addition of a grand portico with Corinthian columns transformed the federal-style Oatlands into a Greek revival building. Brick walls were covered with stucco to resemble stone. *Photography by Wayne Wolfersberger, Nature Is Wild Photography; courtesy Oatlands.*

Exterior view shows the artful
use of greenery from the
Oatlands gardens to decorate
the portico window.

 Cuttings from the extensive grounds decorate
the home's interior and exterior.

House tours during the holiday season are much anticipated. They occur every half-hour from late November through December. Schedules for traditional pre-Christmas candlelight tours are announced.

The "Friends of Oatlands" Holiday Open House takes place right after Thanksgiving. This major event, which kicks off the holiday season, is a time when Oatlands expresses appreciation for key supporters of its mission and many year-round programs. "Members may come to preview the decorations and Santa joins us in the Drawing Room," says executive director Andrea McGimsey.

The play's the thing—even at Christmas—and the Stage Coach Theatre Company ensures that there will be a good one. There might be a rerun of the company's "Jingling All the Way"—a for-laughs Christmas themed cabaret with traditional and "hilarious" carols. Or, perhaps this talented group will present something entirely new in the historic Carriage House (replete with sound of sleigh or carriage bells in the air).

Certainly, the mansion will be beautifully decorated with a theme in mind. Each room of the 1804 mansion is decorated to dazzle. One Christmas, rooms reflected the high-energy glamour of the red-hot Roaring '20s. A later theme was the Fabulous '40s, with decorations reflecting the war years and later the simple elegance of natural items, such as magnolia and boxwood, that Mrs. Eustis might have had in her garden. "Traditionally, greenery included holly, magnolia, running pine and mistletoe—greenery that decorated the house for the Christmas 1894 wedding of Elizabeth Grayson Carter in the Salon," McGimsey says. Elizabeth Grayson was the granddaughter of George Carter and the daughter of his son, also named George.

Architectural details—elaborate
arched overdoor panel and trim,
highly articulated crown molding,
and an elaborate ceiling medallion
enrich the entry foyer.

 Fanciful wire "trees" bedecked
with crystal beads flank a bouquet
of roses on the foyer table.
Around the doorway is a rope of
magnolia leaves.

Framed portraits of horses inspire the "to the hunt" holiday theme. Former owner and resident William Corcoran Eustis considered Oatlands a great place for fox hunting.

Interior decorating is done by Oatlands staff and volunteers. "Occasionally we have a local design firm decorate a room or two," McGimsey says. "Each year we have a theme and we try to decorate the trees according to that theme, using period ornaments or items if we have them. For the past two years, we've made paper chains because that was something done in the early twentieth century. We decorate with live greenery in certain areas of the mansion. This year Damewood Design, a local design firm, decorated the Salon and West Hall with preserved greens, such as boxwood, magnolia, and chestnuts, reminiscent of what Mrs. Eustis would have had in her garden. Typically our garden staff and volunteers make the wreaths and exterior roping. There are no décor re-runs! Every year is a surprise worth waiting for."

 The vividly decorated Christmas tree adds festivity to
the elegant drawing room. Greenery and chunky white
candles decorate the marble mantel.

Gingerbread dolls in the chair and a Santa collection on the mantel add fun to a formal setting. A homemade paper chain decorates the tree.

BEGINNINGS. George Carter, a bachelor and great-grandson of Robert "King" Carter, head of one of Virginia's "first families," began Oatlands in 1798, when he inherited 3,408 acres of land in Loudoun County from his father. He created first a wheat farm, then added other grains, sheep, a gristmill, and saw mill. He successfully petitioned his neighbor, President James Monroe, to establish a post office at Oatlands Mill, and Carter became its first post master. In an age before John Deere tractors and other machinery, farming relied on manual labor. Carter depended on an enslaved labor force to work his lands, harvest the crops, and build a thriving plantation. Prior to the Civil War Oatlands had the largest slave population in Loudoun County. By 1860, just before the start of the Civil War, there were 132 men, women, and children at Oatlands.

Every plantation, of course, has a "big house." George Carter himself probably planned his, basing its design on early nineteenth-century architectural styles found in pattern books. Original plans were for a federal- or Adam-style mansion (with east and west bays flanking a central block). Construction on the Oatlands mansion began in 1803 and continued for about five years. The house was far from finished when the War of 1812 caused a recession that halted work.

By the time he resumed work on his home, Carter had decided to convert his designs to the popular Greek revival style. Red brick walls were covered in stucco scored to look like stone. He added a grand portico replete with Corinthian columns to the mansion face, and half-octagonal staircases at either end. A roof line parapet wall on the front and sides of the building and a cupola emphasized the new design's linearity. Inside (above a full basement), the house had three living floors and an attic. Carter enclosed two corners of his drawing room to create a popular octagon shape.

In 1835, at age fifty-eight, George married Elizabeth Grayson Lewis, widow of Joseph Lewis Jr. (who had been a Congressional representative of Loudoun County). George and Elizabeth Grayson Lewis Carter had two sons, George and Benjamin.

George Carter Sr. died in 1846, at age sixty-nine. Elizabeth and her sons continued to live at the plantation, and she ran it during the Civil War. Her diary records happenings at the plantation shortly before, during, and for a while after that war. She notes the weather, wind direction, livestock transactions, visitors, and trips to Leesburg, She comments about bringing back runaway slaves. She mentions making calico shirts for Confederate volunteers, the encampment of Confederate troops on plantation grounds, troop movements, nearby battles (including the 1861 Battle of Balls Bluff and the 1862 Battle of Seven Pines). She records the ransacking of Oatlands by insolent Yankees. She frequently mentions her son, George Carter Jr., and refers to members of the Grayson, Carter, and other families. Her last entry is dated October 31, 1872. She died in 1885.

In the late 1960s, Grace Carter Beach Barber (a great-granddaughter of Oatlands founder George Carter), sent the estate an account of her mother's remembrances of Christmas at Oatlands. "Through her daughter's words the memories of Elizabeth Grayson Carter are preserved," McGimsey says.

We mostly depended on Mother's Rag Bag for our sewing materials. Much romantic history was buried in that Rag Bag and here we got our inspiration for our best presents. We found bits of satin and velvet, remnants of ancient party clothes given to us mostly by the Boarders. Those mysterious possessions added just the right finishing touch to any Christmas present. The mere opening of the Bag thrilled us and created in each of us, I am sure, a love of finery.

We never had any candles on the tree as Mother was afraid of fire, but we had everything else on it. We had yards of colored paper chains, paper flowers made by us and always lots of the little lady apples strung on red or silver thread, little dolls dressed in finery, colored balls and again yards and yards of popcorn strings as we thought this made the tree look snowy. Our stockings were hung at the foot of our beds so we could open them the minute we opened our eyes.

After the Civil War, George and his wife, Katherine Powell Carter, tried operating a girls' school there. Later, they converted Oatlands to a summer boarding house. Finally, in 1897, the Carter family sold the mansion with 60 acres of land to Stilson Hutchins, founder of the *Washington Post*. Hutchins never lived on the property. Instead, in 1903, the absentee owner sold Oatlands to Mr. and Mrs. William Corcoran Eustis. Mr. Eustis saw the property as a great place for fox hunting. Mrs. Eustis saw the gardens as a challenge. They left the house as it was— true to George Carter's completed design.

The sleigh bed holds an American flag and WWII military jacket. In the box beside the bed are medals. The lone star banner in the window denoted that a household member was serving in the armed forces.

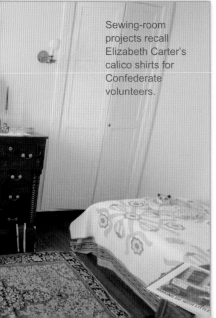

In a sitting room, lest we forget, were early means of speeding communication—a radio, push-button telephone, and typewriter.

Sewing-room projects recall Elizabeth Carter's calico shirts for Confederate volunteers.

GARDEN. George Carter had built a terraced garden, which created flat beds for planting. They had suffered great neglect by the time Mr. and Mrs. Eustis bought the property. Mrs. Eustis devoted herself to restoring the gardens. To the terraces she added boxwood-lined parterres. She planted a rose garden and built a bowling green and reflecting pool. A remarkable collection of statuary includes *The Fawn* at the end of the pool and *Vierge d'Autun*, a memorial to a daughter who died at the age of twenty-four.

 Frosty the Snowman makes himself at home in the tub.

BECOMING A MUSEUM. At Mrs. Eustis' death in 1964, her daughters donated the mansion, furnishings, and estate grounds to the National Trust. The site was declared a National Historic Landmark in 1971. In 1974, the site and the surrounding easements designated as the Oatlands Historic District were listed on the National Register of Historic Places.

 A high second-floor windowsill shows off a collection of miniature Christmas trees.

173

Christmas lights define the house and spell out a cheerful holiday message at the Clinton House Museum. *Photography by Director Kate Johnson, courtesy Clinton House Museum*

A CHRISTMAS COTTAGE
Clinton House

It caught her eye as she and Bill drove by en route to the airport—a red brick house near the University of Arkansas. She noted the for-sale sign. "Sweet looking little house," she recalls saying, but giving it no more thought, as recounted in her book *Living History*.

Before their marriage, Bill Clinton and Hillary Rodham were teaching at the University of Arkansas School of Law in Fayetteville. In his book *My Life*, Bill recalls that, "One day I drove her to the airport for a trip back east. As we were driving down California Drive, we passed a beautiful little jagged brick house set back on a rise with a stone wall bracing up the front yard. There was a for-sale sign in the yard. She remarked on how pretty the place was. After I dropped her off, I checked the house out."

Bill returned to walk through the one-story structure on California Drive (with no idea that in 2010 the street would be named Clinton Drive). He estimated the 1,800-square-foot house to be about 1,100 square feet. The one-bedroom, one-bathroom house had a kitchen with attached breakfast room, a small dining room, and a large screened-in porch (which he thought could double as a three-season guest room). The surprise: "A gorgeous living room that had a beamed ceiling half again as high as the others in the house, a good-looking offset fireplace, and a big bay window," he writes.

— FAYETTEVILLE, ARKANSAS —

No doubt Bill's years in England as a Rhodes Scholar had honed his eye for excellence in architecture. The living room's vaulted ceiling, inglenook fireplace, and story-and-a-half bay window of the 1931 Tudor Revival house were deal makers. On August 11, 1975, with a down-payment of $3,000 (keeping monthly mortgage payments at $174), he purchased the house for $17,200. Previous residents of this charming house had been H. H. Taylor, owner of the Fayetteville *Daily Leader*, and Gilbert C. Swanson, who founded Swanson Foods in Omaha, Nebraska, with his brother and father. After inventing the TV dinner, Gilbert moved to Fayetteville to run operations for chicken TV dinners (the original dinners were turkey and dressing). Gilbert and his wife Roberta then invented the chicken pot pie while living in the house. "Roberta Fulbright Swanson

was a sister to Senator J. William Fulbright of Fulbright Scholarship fame, a lifelong mentor to Bill, who never knew that Fulbright's sister had lived in his home until I was able to tell him in 2010," says Kate Johnson, director of the Clinton House Museum. "So the history of the house reveals a unique 'degrees of separation' connection."

Bill moved some furnishings in ("so that the place wasn't totally bare") and when Hillary returned from her trip back east, he proposed (for the fourth time). "Bill told me in 2010 that he'd bought an old iron bed from the Salvation Army for five dollars to put in the bedroom," Johnson says. Hillary recalled (in *Living History*) that Bill picked her up at the airport and asked, "Do you remember that house you liked? Well, I bought it, so now you'd better marry me because I can't live in it by

 Opposite
Distinctive features such as the
stepped chimney and the handsome
two-story bay window reflect the
work of an accomplished architect
and caught the eye of Hillary as she
and Bill were driving past.

 Wreaths on doors and ropes of
greenery greet visitors to the Clinton
house at Christmastime.

 A large Christmas tree decorates the living room, which contains materials from the Clintons' political campaigns The bedroom (*right*) also boasts a beautifully bedecked tree.

myself." The irrefutable argument—and a tour of the interior whose kitchen, she noted "needed a lot of work"—carried the day. Bill Clinton and Hillary Rodham were married in that gorgeous living room on October 11, 1976. Bill recalls that "Hillary wore an old-fashioned Victorian lace dress that I loved." The story is that the night before the wedding, Hillary's mother persuaded her that she needed a wedding dress. The two went shopping in the only store still open—Dillard's, an Arkansas-based company with headquarters in Little Rock. The lovely Jessica McClintock dress cost $53, and its replica is displayed in the living room.

The next several months were busy times for the Clintons. Bill ran for Arkansas State attorney general and won. Despite their busy schedules, he found time to tackle a DIY project—tiling the fireplace surround. Hillary describes it as a weekend project that became a monthlong one. That tile is still in place. Bill also tried his hand at wallpapering the breakfast nook. "Hillary took a picture of his finished product and then told him to take it down," Johnson says. "That picture hangs in the nook." Hillary told Bill that manual labor was not his forte. Clearly, politics was. Home again after a summer of campaigning, Bill did a recapitulation of his past three years: taught ten law courses, campaigned for office twice, and managed a presidential campaign. He decided he had loved every minute of it, "regretting only the time it took me away from . . . that little house at 930 California Drive that brought Hillary and me so much joy," he writes in *My Life*.

 Bill and Hillary were married in the living room. Today, a replica of her wedding dress is on display there.

The Clintons lived in their home through only two Christmases. No one seems to remember much about that first holiday season, which followed a demanding three years. Johnson says: "It's extremely unlikely that they decorated or did anything special for Christmas. They were a pretty 'no frills' couple. Bill's mom and brother lived three hours away in Hot Springs, and they probably spent the holiday with them. However, Hillary comes from a close-knit family and her brothers were attending the University of Arkansas in

 A lighted tree and brightly colored cabinets enliven the kitchen.

 Every room seems to have a Christmas tree and every room is chock-full of material about the Clintons, beginning with their years as students.

Fayetteville. Since Hugh and Tony would have gone 'back home' for Christmas between the college semesters, it's just as likely they might have all traveled together to Hillary's hometown of Chicago with Bill in tow."

In November 1976, Bill became the attorney general of the state of Arkansas, and they moved from the home in December. They owned it until 1982, and during that time Hillary's brothers lived in the house. "The Clintons still recognized Fayetteville as their home, and thus the house their permanent address," Johnson says. "They would even come back to Fayetteville to vote. It was after they moved from Fayetteville, when Bill was involved in politics and after Chelsea was born in 1980, that they participated in the pomp and circumstance of the holiday season. True to Southern tradition, they would have had a 'real' tree. Being allergic to 'all things green,' including garland, wreaths, and trees, Bill often suffered from a stuffy nose, watery eyes, and the familiar puffiness under his eyes," Johnson says. When they moved to Little Rock, the state capital. Bill and Hillary Rodham Clinton were on their way into American history books.

The house became a museum in 2005, and today Christmas is a special time on Clinton Drive. Museum highlights include rarely seen memorabilia of Clinton's early political career, including campaigns for US House of Representatives and attorney general, Johnson says. "Clinton's earliest political speeches, showcasing his unique style that would eventually be discovered by millions around the globe, are shown there, and a time line puts into perspective Bill's and Hillary's years in Fayetteville, where the Clintons taught law in the mid-'70s. A real treat—even in winter—is to explore the First Ladies Garden on the museum grounds. It features the favorite flowers of America's first ladies from Martha Washington to Michele Obama."

 Former President Bill Clinton stops by.

 A street lamp banner marks the place where Bill and Hillary were married and lived while teaching at the nearby University of Arkansas, Fayetteville.

Candlelight tours of the 1863 Shriver house, authentically restored to its original state, begin on Thanksgiving evening and continue through the last Saturday before Christmas Day. *Photography by Del Gudmestad, courtesy the Shriver House Museum*

A CIVIL WAR CHRISTMAS
Shriver House Museum

Traditionally, candlelight Christmas tours of the Shriver House Museum begin on Thanksgiving evening and continue Saturday evenings through the last Saturday before Christmas. To open the door and walk into the Shrivers' 1860s home, which has been faithfully restored to look as it did in 1863, offers a glimpse of a bygone era. One experiences the warmth of the season in an old-fashioned style that ignites the spirit of the season.

George Washington Shriver was born on July 27, 1836, on a prosperous farm about 8 miles southeast of Gettysburg. In addition to traditional farming, George's father manufactured liquor for sale. When his father died in the fall of 1852, George inherited the family's 200-acre farm, large barn, distillery, and more than 3,000 gallons of liquor. Three years later, in January 1855, eighteen-year-old George and eighteen-year-old Hettie Weikert, who lived on a nearby farm, were married.

— GETTYSBURG, PENNSYLVANIA —

In spring 1860, George sold a portion of his farm. For $290, he bought property on Baltimore Street near the center of Gettysburg. Plans called for building a home for his family and opening a new business: Shriver's Saloon & Ten-Pin Alley. The saloon was in the cellar while the two-lane Ten-Pin (bowling) Alley was in a building behind the house. In August 1861, construction was finished and the business ready to open. By this time, George and Hettie had two daughters—Sadie, five years old and Mollie, who was three. At age twenty-five, George had sold off the remainder of his farm for $3,420. With money in the bank and a good business, the future looked promising.

 An open door with beautiful sidelights and over-lights invites visitors into the gracious foyer, where seasonal greenery ropes festoon the door and ceiling.

 Opposite
A candle in the window—a beacon in the night and an ages-old symbol of welcome—is especially heartening at Christmastime.

 A wreath, ancient symbol of continuity, brightens a window.

 A holiday table top is decorated with sweet treats, including a clear candy rabbit.

 Stockings hanging from the mantel could be simple, unadorned. The tabletop tree is decorated with miniature American flags, a popular Victorian expression.

 "Crackers" made a crackling noise when guests pulled them apart to find surprise gifts inside.

 A portrait of Civil War President Lincoln is decorated for the candlelight tour season.

 A kerosene lamp illuminates a Victorian mirror.

 The gift shop offers a wealth of items carefully selected to reflect the period of the house and the Christmas season.

 A single candle emphasizes shelter against the cold and snowy winter.

the battle of Gettysburg. That evidence included Civil War medical supplies, live Civil War ammunition, holes cut through the walls by Confederate sharpshooters, and bullet holes in exterior walls. The most amazing discovery was found 143 years after the Battle of Gettysburg when a forensics expert used a luminol-like chemical to reveal the presence of mass amounts of blood which corroborated the accounts of Confederates being shot while in the Shrivers' attic during the conflict.

When George enlisted in 1861, he and Hettie believed the war would be over in a few months and George would be home by Christmas. Instead, George had been away for two years when Confederate soldiers crossed the Mason-Dixon Line and entered Pennsylvania. On June 26, 1863, a band of Confederate soldiers passed through the town, and six days later the battle of Gettysburg began, early in the morning on July 1.

On the Candlelight Tour, museum docents describe what happened to Hettie and her children when Hettie decided to leave Gettysburg and walk 3 miles, through the middle of the battle, to seek safety at her childhood farm. But she found her family's farm overrun by thousands of Union soldiers and her parents' home being used as a hospital. Docents describe her walk back to Gettysburg over a battlefield where more than 5,000 soldiers had been killed. Scattered on the ground were rifles, swords, canteens, belts, shoes, knapsacks, blankets, bits of uniforms, body parts, and damaged tools and implements, as well as more than 7,000 dead mules and horses. The stories are of graphic scenes— not music to the ears, and no substitute for the traditional hymns and carols of a peacetime Christmas.

Five months after the Battle of Gettysburg, George Shriver was granted a four-day furlough. He spent Christmas with Hettie, Sadie, and Mollie, who had prepared for the holiday in anxious anticipation of his return. On Christmas Eve, a candle-laden, 4-foot Christmas tree was in its place of honor on the parlor table. A fire warmed the handsome room, which was decorated with handmade holiday greenery. After stringing popcorn for the tree and hanging their stocking on the mantel, Sadie and Mollie set out milk and cookies in anticipation of a visit from Santa Claus and his reindeer. Christmas offered a few moments of cheer to brighten the lives of those who stayed at home and of the soldiers who, like George Shriver, could come home for this holy day.

But the War between the States was beginning and George volunteered to serve in Cole's Cavalry.

No architectural changes were made to the Shrivers' home until the early 1900s, when two additions were added to the back of the house to provide indoor plumbing. In January 1996, after being abandoned for nearly thirty years, restoration work on the house began. There was no electricity, window panes were missing, and the roof had a serious leak. What had happened in the intervening years to the Shriver family and to their house? Discovered in walls and beneath floorboards and hearths during the restoration were artifacts that provided clues: children's toys, a child's shoe (which was put inside the wall of the house during construction to bring good luck), corset stays, letters, pictures, and much more. Other discoveries provided evidence that the Shriver family witnessed and suffered dreadful things during

A MODEL CHRISTMAS
The Ford House

Edsel Ford's Model A car revolutionized America's automobile industry, and Edsel Ford went right on creating cars with sophisticated streamlined silhouettes and eye-catching colors. An only child, Edsel was Henry Ford's son and heir to the Ford Motor Company. He grew up with cars, began working at the Ford Motor Company in 1912, and became vice president in 1917. In 1915, at age twenty-two, Edsel was named to the Ford Motor Company's board of directors. In 1916, he became company secretary and in 1919 was named company president.

Edsel and his childhood friend, Eleanor Lowthian Clay, married in 1916. They met at dance class when they were in their late teens. By 1925, parents of four children (Henry II, Benson, Josephine, and

Photography by Jeff Sauger, courtesy of Ford House

William), they decided to build a home in Grosse Pointe Shores. Work began in 1926 and the house was finished two years later. In this picturesque home, they raised their family. Today, it is one of America's most remarkable house museums, showing how one of America's most prominent families lived during what might be called the "age of the automobile." During this time, owning a car became commonplace and speed increasingly important. Christmas is a wonderful time to visit. Holiday decorations keep Eleanor's traditions, beginning with a 15-foot-high Christmas tree in the grand gallery. Key rooms of their sixty-room house are decorated for the season.

— GROSSE POINTE SHORES, MICHIGAN —

Christmas today includes a number of exciting events. The estate grounds, the visitor center, and the house provide a magical setting for family fun and making memories. Leading up to Christmas Day, children can meet Santa, tell him their wishes, and snap a photo together during a personal meet-and-greet. Visitors of various ages and interests participate in guided do-it-yourself workshops on gardening, craft projects, and entertaining. There is also music, delectable dining, hot beverages, and beautiful wintry landscapes.

 Edsel and Eleanor Ford's sixty-room house was designed to look like an assemblage of Cotswolds cottages. *Photography courtesy Edsel & Eleanor Ford House*

 Christmas is very much for children at Ford House. *Photograph by John F. Martin, courtesy of Ford House*

A tour of Eleanor and Edsel's house treats visitors to the warmth and beauty of the home and stories of the Ford family's lives and holiday traditions. Select rooms feature beautiful seasonal decorations. Eleanor's iconic flocked Christmas tree is extraordinary with its original ornaments in pinks and purples. Outdoor events are geared toward the entire family with storytelling, games, and tasty holiday treats

ABOUT THE HOUSE. Edsel and Eleanor built their final residence, with its 3,000 feet of lake frontage, on about 125 scenic acres (now eighty-seven) at Gaukler Point on Lake St. Clair, in Grosse Pointe Shores, northeast of Detroit. They chose architect Albert Kahn to design their house. For inspiration, the Fords and Kahn traveled to England. Enchanted by the cottages of the Cotswolds, they settled on a design that resembles a collection of cottages. The final design was a 30,000-square-foot structure with sixty rooms, including a kitchen, butler's pantry, and flower room where the staff worked.

It took a year to complete the shell, with its Briarhill sandstone (from Ohio) exterior. The roof was made from stone in Europe by craftsmen from England, making it authentic, not just authentic looking. Shingle sizes decrease in size as they approach the roof peak—exactly as Cotswolds originals. English craftsmen installed the roof and were brought back whenever repairs were needed.

 The tall tree in the main hallway is decorated in custom teardrop-shaped ornaments.

The 1600s staircase is from Lyvedon
Old Bield Manor, Northamptonshire.

 Opposite
A Christmas tree on the landing can be admired from floors above and below and from outside the window.

 The Christmas tree in the drawing room keeps good company with the Louis XV and Louis XVI furnishings.

The interior build-out took two years, since many of the materials were imported. Six old English manor houses yielded antique wood paneling, fireplaces, and a staircase. Records show that the hooded chimney piece for the gallery came from Wollaston Hall in Worcestershire. Paneling for the dining room came from a house in Upminster, a London suburb. Library paneling (and the Caen stone chimney piece) came from Deane Park, Northamptonshire. The study's ca. 1585 wooden overmantel came from Heronden Hall, Kent. The Morning Room walls are paneled in eighteenth-century pine from Spitalfields. The ca. 1600 staircase from Lyvedon Old Bield Manor, Northamptonshire, was cut to fit its new home.

One of the most interesting materials in the house is the German silver used for kitchen counters. In an age before stainless steel, it was deemed durable. Great attention was given to every interior detail. Each of the ten plaster ceilings in key public rooms boasts a unique, intricate tracery pattern. In other noteworthy details, Edsel Ford's study is lined with Elizabethan paneling. Photographs show his boats (used to travel down Lake St. Clair, the Detroit River, and the Rouge River) and many other subjects.

The dining room's japanned (English) corner cabinet dates from 1750–75. The drawing room furniture is Louis XV and Louis XVI. The entrance hall staircase is ca. 1600 English. Josephine's bedroom features an American flag that accompanied Admiral Richard Byrd on one of his journeys and was flown over the North Pole.

Among the more fascinating rooms are those remodeled by Walter Dorwin Teague in the 1930s in art moderne style. An industrial designer, Teague was known for office interiors, corporate buildings, cars, trains, and planes. Edsel Ford had hired him to design pavilions and displays for world's fairs,

 Brilliant red berries and seasonal greenery highlight the mantel in the dining room. In the corner is a japanned English corner cabinet, ca. 1750–75.

 Above/Opposite
Several views of the library show the extraordinary Caen stone chimney piece and wall paneling from Dean Park, Northamptonshire.

A 15-foot tree in the gallery continues an Eleanor
Ford tradition. The plaster ceilings in ten key
public rooms feature intricate tracery patterns.

auto shows, and dealer showrooms. For the Ford's home,
Teague created the first floor Modern Room, which featured
indirect lighting (new at the time) and leather wall panels in
a sophisticated taupe color. A curved niche wall was fitted
with vertical strips of mirror. Teague also designed the bed
and sitting room suites for the three sons and a game room.
All these rooms incorporated typical Teague innovations,
such as custom streamlined furniture in exotic hardwoods,
copper and brass and bronze metallic finishes, and plastic-
topped tables with built-in radios. In Henry Ford II's bathroom,
he covered the walls and shower stall in glass. Bedroom walls
are industrial glass called Vitrolite made at the Ford glass
plant; the shower stall is chrome and clear glass.

Furnishings throughout the house include countless
authentic antiques carefully chosen by Edsel and Eleanor, who
were serious collectors. At Eleanor's direction, following her
death, important pieces were donated to the Detroit Institute
of Arts. Reproductions of paintings by Renoir, Degas, Cezanne,
and Van Gogh replace the originals. Some original works
remain, including two Cezannes and a Diego Rivera.

Famed landscape architect Jens Jensen designed the grounds
in his trademark naturalistic style. A much-contested rose
garden hides behind native bushes in an inconspicuous location.
Among the garden structures is Josephine's three-quarter-scale
playhouse, a 1930 gift from her grandmother, Clara Ford.

After Edsel Ford's death 1943, Eleanor Ford continued to live there. When she handed the house over in trust in the 1970s, she provided $15 million dollars for its maintenance. Following her death in 1976, the house was left for "the benefit of the public." It is listed on the National Register of Historic Places, and the estate is a recognized National Historic Landmark. Thousands tour the house throughout the year, but Christmas remains a favorite season for visiting.

 White fairy lights transform the garden for strolling during the Winter Wonderland Weekend, an event designed for families.

 Artful lighting makes bundling up for a rose garden tour worthwhile.

 In 1930, Clara Ford gave her granddaughter Josephine the three-quarter-scale playhouse, a charming stop during the holiday season. *Photography by John F. Martin, courtesy of Ford House*

Mathias Fassel purchased the original two-room Fassel-Roeder house in 1876 and enlarged it. *Photography by architect David Strahan*

A PIONEER CHRISTMAS
Fassel - Roeder House

When Mathias Fassel bought his house in late 1876, it sat directly behind the Main Street shop where he made wheels and axles and assembled and repaired buggies and wagons. That shop is gone, but the house remains on its original site. Today, it is called the Fassel-Roeder House because Anna Fassel, the daughter of Mathias and Maria Fassel, married William Roeder Jr., and the Roeder family was the last to live there. The Fassels remodeled what had been a one-room butcher shop. At first, they added a large kitchen, closing in a window to make it a kitchen shelf. The original room became the bedroom. The attic was the children's bedroom. Later, the Fassels added two rooms to the front of the building. Later, the partition between the two front rooms was removed and the one large room became a spacious parlor. They also added a porch spanning the front of the house.

— FREDERICKSBURG, TEXAS —

Family members who lived on nearby farms used the house as a gathering place when they came to town to see a doctor, shop, attend church, and so on. "Occasionally, before there were funeral homes, services for relatives were held in the house," says archivist Evelyn Weinheimer, citing Mathias Fassel's daughter, Lina Dupray, when she was interviewed for a story for the *Fredericksburg Standard*, a local newspaper, in 1956.

 The charming front porch trimmed in "carpenter's Gothic" millwork is a later addition to the original house, which sat behind Fassel's wheelwright shop. Architect David Strahan sketched a porch detail.

 Bits of cedar branches decorate windowsills in the parlor. Fredericksburg's West Main Street can be glimpsed through the front room windows.

Originally the parlor was a two-room addition to the front. The dividing wall was removed to create a spacious parlor. The tall case "grandfather" clock belonged to the F. W. Lange family. The hand-pegged wardrobes in this room once belonged to members of the family of Baron Meusebach who led settlers to found Fredericksburg.

Decorations were almost always
handmade from whatever materials
were available.

White plaster dresses up native stone walls in the parlor. Atop the upright piano, a kerosene lamp sheds light on handcrafted polychrome nativity figures.

There are several items of interest in this old stone house, one of several structures that now comprise the Pioneer Museum. In the parlor is a large grandfather clock from the F. W. Lange family, and hand-pegged wardrobes from the Marshall-Meusebach families. Meusebach, of course, refers to Baron Meusebach, who led the first band of German settlers from New Braunfels to establish farms and the village of Fredericksburg. The parlor also contains a music box or polyphon made in 1885 in Leipzig, Germany (it could be played by inserting a dime), a very old telephone, and a treadle sewing machine. The bedroom holds an early caned-seat wheelchair, a child's crib, and other artifacts.

 The parlor's cedar Christmas tree would have been cut on the farm and brought to town. Decorations included hand-strung popcorn chains and ornaments crafted from scraps of paper and cloth.

Antique toy trains join wrapped gifts
beneath the tree.

 The master bedroom is furnished with many
old artifacts, including a child's crib and
cane-back wheelchair.

 A cedar-post arbor shades one rear entrance, while a covered porch protects the kitchen entrance. From inside the kitchen there is a view of the Walton-Smith log cabin, one of several preserved homes that make up the Pioneer Museum.

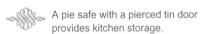 A pie safe with a pierced tin door provides kitchen storage.

THE KITCHEN is perhaps the most fascinating room, with its kitchen cabinets dating back to 1859. Wall-hung and base kitchen cabinets with countertops that we know today did not become commonplace until the 1920s. Before then, storage cabinets (forerunners of the Hoosier cabinets) held foodstuffs, cooking supplies, and utensils. The kitchen also contains an early butter churn—a glass jar fitted with a blade turned by a handle attached to the lid—an old coffee grinder, and a large wood stove. The wall color—a pleasant and lively blue—was achieved by adding bluing (a laundry agent that whitens fabrics) with a dye called Prussian blue (ferric hexacyanoferrate) to whitewash (a low-cost type of paint made from slaked lime, calcium hydroxide) and chalk (whiting).

 A butter churn was made from a hand-cranked paddle and glass jar.

 Perhaps the most remarkable architectural feature is the built-in kitchen cabinetry, ca. 1859. Built-in cabinets did not become a popular feature in American kitchens until the 1920s.

 The cheerful blue "paint" on the wall was
made by adding laundry "bluing" to
whitewash.

 Opposite
A large iron cook stove occupies a
kitchen niche.

At Christmastime, the house is decorated much the same as it would have been when the Fassels lived there. The big tree in the parlor is a cedar, which probably would have been cut from the farm and brought to town. In Texas it was common to use cedars as Christmas trees, and the branches were used to decorate windows and doorways. Throughout the Fassel-Roeder house, evergreen branches, pine cones, and berries add holiday color to windowsills.

"Tree decorations were made from whatever was at hand," Weinheimer says. Most common were popcorn chains, paper flowers, paper chains made of stiff colored paper, intricate paper ornaments, decorated cookies, candy and nuts wrapped in bright scraps of paper, ribbons, bits of glass and metal, polished fruit, and homemade candles."

A large cupboard called a shrank holds china and glassware. A glass front shows off a pretty teapot. A peach basket painted white and filled with cedar branches adds seasonal color and fragrance to the kitchen.

Wrapped presents and antique toys surround the tree base. "Young children were told not to open the door and could not peek through the keyhole," she adds. "They were told that the Weihnachtsman (Father Christmas) might bring presents that evening. But they never saw him, although they sometimes thought they heard him moving about. They were not allowed to see the tree until Christmas Eve or Christmas morning."

No one knows exactly how the Fassels observed Christmas, but we can speculate by observing the early German traditions. "Germans placed a candle in the window so the Christ Child, who might be wandering in the dark streets, would know he was welcome to enter," says Weinheimer. She cites a passage from *Coffee in the Gourd*, in which the author Julia Estill describes a Texas Hill Country Christmas among the Germans.

On December 24, a Santa Claus comes to some homes. He enters about the time the candles on the cedar tree are lighted and the home circle is gathered in the "best room." Every child is then asked to pray. This is the little petition the children lisp at bedtime: "*Ich bin klien; mein Herz ist rein; soll*

niemand drin wohnen als Jesus allein." (I am small; my heart is pure; no one shall abide there save Jesus alone.) Satisfied, Santa leaves an apple or orange with each child and repairs to the neighboring house if the children have all responded with the prayer. But woe to the unruly youngster, usually a sophisticated boy, who refuses to pray! He is soundly rapped with the huge stick Santa conceals under his mantle.

"Today, Saint Nick, the jollier version of Father Christmas, is recalled at Kinderfest, an event held at Pioneer Museum," Weinheimer says. "Children ages ten and under come to hang stockings over the large fireplace in the Kammlah House (next door to the Fassel-Roeder House), then go to the main building to listen to stories, sing songs, and do a craft activity. The children return to the Kammlah House to collect the treats Saint Nicholas leaves in their stockings." *Kinderfest* occurs each year on the Saturday that falls closest to December 6.

For adults there is a candlelight tour and a December 26 event, *Zweite Weihnachten*, or second Christmas, which is an open house with refreshments.

On the kitchen side of the house is a garden with herbs that the household would have used.

Sage

Mexican Mint Marigold

The late-nineteenth-century Queen Anne house in Owen Sound, Ontario, Canada was the boyhood home of Billy Bishop, Canada's top World War I flying ace who was awarded medals by Canada, Great Britain, and France. *Photography by Heather Hughes, courtesy Bishop House: Museum Archives and National Historic Site*

UP, UP, AND AWAY FOR A MERRY HOLIDAY
Bishop House Museum

To visit William Avery "Billy" Bishop's birthplace and boyhood home at Christmas is to see the site where Billy first took to the air. As a boy, he built his own wooden-crate-and-cardboard aircraft, going airborne off the house's back roof. His sister dug him out of the wreckage unscathed, and he went on to adult derring-do. Today, the Bishop House in Owen Sound, Ontario, Canada, is a museum dedicated to the memory of Canada's top World War I flying ace, an international aviation hero. The handsome, brick two-and-a-half-story Queen Anne Bishop House is typical of a late-nineteenth-century middle-class Canadian home. Distinctive architectural features include its steeply pitched roof, front and side gables, and large wraparound front porch with handsome columns. Until 1987, Bishop's extended family owned this house. Remarkably, it retains original hardwood floors and the original layout—so visitors can see Billy's boyhood bedroom.

— OWEN SOUND, ONTARIO, CANADA —

 A decorated entry foyer staircase welcomes visitors to the annual Victorian Christmas Open House.

 When Billy was a boy, the Christmas stockings would have hung on the mantel in the master bedroom.

 In the Victorian "more is better" spirit, the front parlor is gaily decorated with ropes of greenery. On display is a collection of period children's toys.

Every November, the public is invited to a Victorian Christmas Open House. "When Louise Bishop (Billy's sister) was lady of the house, stockings were hung on the fireplace in the master bedroom," says Mindy Gill-Johnson, museum curator of collections. "Christmas morning, after breakfast, presents were opened under the tree. Then it was time to visit family. There was always a live tree." The museum staff places a tree in the front parlour and dining room and hangs wreaths and garlands. Porch columns are festooned with ribbons and more garland.

During the Victorian Christmas celebrations, a few toys that belonged to the Bishop children are displayed, including a wooden boat pull toy, toy sewing machine, doll's travel trunk, and cast iron Hansen carriage. There are also two ceramic Santa ornaments that belonged to the Bishop family. The toys are placed under the tree in the front parlor and the Santas are displayed on the dining room mantel."

While the decorations are spirit-lifting, it is the artifacts of Bishop's military career that dazzle. An outdoor plaque cites his shooting down of seventy-two enemy aircraft in WW I and leading "daring missions" with "conspicuous bravery" into hostile territory. A long list of decorations includes the Victoria Cross and the Distinguished Service Order (DSO). In addition to decorations by Canada and Great Britain, Bishop was awarded the French Legion d'honneur (Chevalier) and Croix de guerre (2 Bronze Palms). After his October 1917 marriage to Margaret Eaton Burden, he was assigned to the British War Mission in

 Small photographs of family members were a popular Victorian ornament.

Washington, DC, to help the Americans build an air force. While stationed there, he wrote an autobiography titled *Winged Warfare*. In WW II, Bishop served as honorary air marshal with the Royal Canadian Air Force in Ottawa. Bishop, of course, did more than merely pilot planes. He is credited with helping to establish the British Commonwealth Air Training Plan.

In the museum are uniforms, medals, photos, and model airplanes from Bishop and other Canadians who fought in the air during World War I and World War II. In 1928, when Bishop visited Berlin, he was guest of honor at a meeting of an association of German air aces, who made Bishop an honorary member.

Toys that belonged to the Bishop children are displayed around the tree in the front parlor.

The weather outside might be gloomy, but inside the dining room is aglow. Standing displays and cases tell the Bishop story.

Ever adventurous, Bishop offered his aid during the Korean War, but the RCAF refused the services of the ailing aviator. Bishop died at his winter home in Palm Beach, Florida, at age sixty-two, and his ashes were interred in the cemetery at Owen Sound. A funeral service with full military honors was held in Toronto, and a memorial service took place in Bristol, England.

To visit the Bishop House is to be inspired by a life lived with singular focus, real purpose, and a strong sense of duty.

 Two ceramic Santa ornaments that belonged to the Bishops are displayed on the dining room mantel during the Victorian Christmas Open House.

 A Bishop family photograph album is open for viewing. Other rooms are devoted to illustrating the Bishop family history in general and the extraordinary life of William Avery "Billy" Bishop.

 The dining room fireplace, in the Victorian style, incorporates beautifully carved woodwork with a "built-in" framed mirror over the mantel. Handcrafted arts and crafts tiles add a decorative note to the fireplace surround.

A HAPPY HOLIDAYS HOUSE
Historic Britton House

"Yuletide: Holiday Time at Bayou Bend" is an annual tradition eagerly anticipated. One often hears about a great old house that is about to be demolished, but at the very last moment a hero steps in and rescues it. That's about how it was in 1985, when the decrepit Britton house in Troy, Missouri, was going on the auction block. Troy native Clay Marsh and his partner, noted antique dealer Chet Breitwieser, had moved from Arrow Rock, Missouri, in 1984 to help Clay's widowed mother manage the family business. Successful preservationists of several old houses, they had noticed the house that occupied three city lots at the corner of Main and Boone in the heart of downtown Troy. "She (the house) sat there looking like Miss Haversham in her tattered wedding gown," Breitwieser says. "We toured the house, noticing original flooring, mantels, glass in the transoms, chair and stair railings—a diamond in the rough. We were pleasantly surprised

to find the vast majority of original details intact as the house had been divided into apartments at the turn of the twentieth century." Marsh and Breitwieser had masonry, engineering, and construction experts examine the structure, which was declared sound. After estimating the restoration cost and devising a budget, they decided to bid on the house at auction.

— TROY, MISSOURI —

The successful bidder was a local developer who envisioned moving his home and business to the highly visible location. "But when he showed it to his lovely wife the next day," Breitwieser says, "she declared that she would never live *in that dump*." (Or words to that effect.) The developer called Marsh and Breitwieser, suggesting that they buy it for $1,000 above the price he had paid. "That was $36,000. I believe," says Breitwieser. "We were both passionate about federal period architecture, so we decided to forge ahead. We bought Britton House, the oldest residence in Troy and one of the oldest in Lincoln County, and set about restoring it with the professional help of two architects, Robert Kuda and Bart Berneking."

 Christmas finery makes the 1832 federal-style Britton House merry and bright. *Photography courtesy Brian Farmer*

 Opposite
The house was originally restored by Clay Marsh and Chet Breitwieser.

Greenery rope and giant pine cones add rich neutral colors and textures to the staircase banister, which is original to the house.

Breitwieser says that he and Marsh spent the first eight months getting vines off the exterior, securing doors and windows, and updating plumbing and electricity. "We were fortunate to have completed the majority of the restoration work with the enthusiastic support of many local contractors and businesses," he says. "We researched paint colors through Hechler Hardware by sending scrapings to Benjamin Moore color experts who recommended appropriate colors from the company's historic color collection." Windows were removed and restored by a Hannibal, Missouri, company.

A period-appropriate round walnut table and chairs take center stage in the dining room. Mantels and flooring are original.

A Victorian chest in the corner is decorated
with an antique jug and evergreen "bouquet."

 Evergreen boughs, berries, and ribbon are items the original owners might have used to decorate for Christmas.

Years later, Lorene Creech, a dear friend and noted area philanthropist, offered to purchase the house and deed it to the Lincoln County Historical and Archaeological Society. At the sale in 1996, an endowment gift of $10,000 was applied toward its maintenance.

Creech then established a nine-member Britton House board of governors, a division of the Lincoln County Historical and Archeological Society that now owned the house. Two years later, Creech's friend Glenna Spencer Udre enhanced the grounds with proceeds from an endowment—hence the name Glenna's Garden. People's Bank & Trust Company became a corporate sponsor in 1996 and continues to support the house. Other area supporters include Toyota-Bodine Aluminum, the Troy Convention & Visitors Bureau, Troy Furniture, B&B Electric, Flynn Drilling, Worsley Construction, and Snow Hill Nursery. Thanks to the generous support of all, the transformation from eyesore to show-stopper is remarkable. Now, Britton House and Glenna's Garden is a hospitable gathering place for the entire community and a destination for visitors.

A drop-leaf table would have provided a handy work surface in the early kitchen. The child's high chair is from the period.

THE ARCHITECTURE. The house that Sherman Cottle built in 1832 was a clapboard structure in a simple, classic federal style, essentially a cube that emphasizes verticality, symmetry, and restrained surface ornamentation. Square columns terminating in a flat frieze support the roof of the entry porch. Windows are twelve-over-twelve (panes), double-hung style. Chimneys on each side serve fireplaces in four rooms—two on either side of a center hall. The exterior doors on the first floor and second floor (which opens onto the balcony above the porch) have transoms that admit light and air into the interior. It is a handsome, dignified, comfortable house.

Inside, as Breitwieser noted, each of the four fireplaces have their original mantels. Floors are the original pit-sawn, inch-thick, random-width oak planks. Exterior doors were not fitted with locks until later, but the staircase was designed with a "burglar's step" (a step near the bottom with a built-in-creak to arouse the sleeping household), which remains. The original, large brass skeleton key to the front door rim lock was found behind the parlor mantel during restoration.

IN THE BEGINNING. Cottle's house became Britton House when James H. Britton bought the house and added on to it. The 1850 records failed to show there was an existing structure but referred to the property as Britton House.

The colorful Britton, a Virginian, moved to Troy and became a merchant, state representative, clerk of the Missouri House of Representatives, and postmaster of Troy before moving to St. Louis in 1857. There, in 1875, he became the twenty-third mayor of St. Louis. He served for about thirty days—until allegations of ballot stuffing and a recount removed him. It's possible that "Cottle Home" would have been a more reputable name, since Cottle is a respected name in Lincoln County. Sherman Cottle's great-great-great-grandson, John Cottle, is sheriff of Lincoln County.

Another favorite story is that the young Britton was bitten by the California gold fever bug while laying the limestone base for the house. He left for California and stayed away so long that after his parents died and he returned to claim his inheritance, no one recognized him. He could not prove his identity until a doctor stepped up to examine the man's scarred arm—he had treated it when Britton injured it while laying the limestone foundation.

Clay Marsh (who passed away in 2007) and Chet Breitwieser knew well that local lore and history are important to every town. Historic house museums like Britton House encapsulate that history and are a visual reminder of the trials and triumphs of earlier citizens. They offer learning opportunities for contemporary citizens to preserve and contribute to the rich history of the house and town. They educate and inspire in a most entertaining way—most thrillingly at Christmas, the most magical time of the year.

 Blue and white crockery echo the blue trim in the kitchen. Original wall colors were identified in collaboration with Benjamin Moore color consultants.

The kitchen table holds a bounty of items baked for holiday entertaining. A kerosene lamp is a reminder of pre-electricity days in the house.

This modest living room was probably typical of houses in Midland, Texas, during the time that future US President George W. Bush lived here from age five to nine. Furnishings are not original to the Bush family occupancy. *Photography courtesy the George W. Bush Childhood Home*

WEST TEXAS WELCOME
George W. Bush Childhood Home

The house at 1412 West Ohio Street is ordinary, but the family that resided there from 1951 to 1955 is not. Their accomplishments exemplify the uniquely American idea that the pursuit of happiness through hard work, dedication, and commitment to public service will be rewarded.

Built in 1940, the 1,100-square-foot house is similar to the post-WWII ranch-style houses that sprang up across the nation. Two additions increased the size to 1,497 square feet by the time George and Barbara Bush, who had moved from Connecticut to Texas in 1948, purchased it in 1951 for $9,000. From this modest house came two United States presidents, two governors, a first lady, an ambassador, and a CIA director—all members of the family of George H. W. Bush, who became the forty-first president of the United States.

— MIDLAND, TEXAS —

A Christmas tree stands in a niche near the sunroom, glimpsed through an open door.

 In the pine-paneled dining room, recessed shelves hold Bush family photographs. Family memorabilia is on display throughout the room. On a sideboard is a snapshot of an adult George W. Bush and his father, George H. W. Bush—both US presidents (see following page).

Added to the National Register of Historic Places in 2004, the West Ohio Street house was bought for $40,000, restored to its 1950s condition, and opened as a museum in April 2006. It preserves the childhood home of the eldest son, George Walker Bush, who moved with his parents and sister Robin (born December 1949 while the family was in California) into the house in 1951. He was five years old. Fifty years later, in 2001, George W. Bush became the forty-third US president.

Paul St. Hilaire, executive director, describes Midland, Texas, as it was when George W. was growing up there: "It was an idyllic place—a small town with small town values. Families went to church and supported one another. Friends and families spent time together, talking while their children played. The children climbed fences, ran through lawn sprinklers, went to Scout meetings, played sandlot ball. Children pretty much had the run of the town. They could ride their bikes downtown. Young George, early on a baseball enthusiast, recalls riding his bike to a neighbor's house to see the first issue of Sports Illustrated."

Midland was idyllic in many ways for both children and parents. George H. W. Bush had come to Midland to enter the oil industry. During the years at home on West Ohio Street, two sons—John Ellis Bush (Jeb, February 1953) and Neil (January 1955)—were born. Sadly, Robin died of leukemia in October 1953. Barbara Bush was involved with her growing family and with community affairs.

~~ Young George W. Bush built
a snowman.

~~ This ordinary-looking house was home
to extraordinary occupants: two future
US presidents and two governors.

PUBLIC SERVICE, A BUSH TRADITION. Prescott Bush, father of George H. W. Bush, is considered the founder of the Bush political dynasty. A native of Columbus, Ohio, he graduated from St. George's, a noted college prep school, and went on to Yale, where he was a member of the invitation-only "secret" Skull and Bones club. A successful Wall Street executive banker, he became a United States senator, representing Connecticut from 1952 until 1963.

George Herbert Walker Bush, Prescott's son, attended Phillips Academy and on his eighteenth birthday enlisted in the Navy. He was the youngest fighter pilot when he earned his wings. He flew fifty-eight combat missions, was shot down by the Japanese, rescued, awarded the Distinguished Flying Cross, and returned home to enter Yale. While a student, he and Barbara married in 1945. George W. was born in 1946, and in 1948 the couple and their young son headed to West Texas. The Bush family moved away from West Ohio Street to another Midland home in 1955, where another son (Marvin, 1956) was born. In 1959, the family moved to Houston where their last child, Dorothy (1960), was born. George H. W. Bush entered a life of public service (including serving as CIA director) that led to his presidency.

George W. Bush attended Kincaid High School in Houston before entering Phillips Academy in Andover, Massachusetts. Like his father and grandfather, he graduated from Yale University (1968). He returned to Texas and joined the Texas Air National Guard where, like his father, he became a pilot. In 1975, he earned an MBA from Harvard and returned to Midland to start an oil business. He met and married Laura Welch in 1977 and their twin daughters were born in 1981. He was active in his father's 1988 campaign for the US presidency. In 1989, his childhood love of baseball surfaced when he headed a group of investors to buy the Texas Rangers team. In 1994, George W. became governor of Texas and won a second term in 1998. In 1999, he decided to run for US president and in 2001 became the nation's forty-third president.

The house at 3412 West Ohio is furnished much as it was when George W. was growing up there. "The TV in the living room is the same model (Hoffman) that George H. W. and Barbara received as a Christmas gift from her father while they were in Compton, California," says St. Hilaire. "That happed to be the same day that Robin came home after being born. Barbara's father gave George W. his portable record player for Christmas 1954. An identical one is displayed in his bedroom." These days, the house is decorated for the holidays as it might have been had the Bush family been at home for the holidays, rather than back East with their family. It welcomes those who want to see firsthand what it was like for two future US presidents to live in a seemingly ordinary place.

 Young George's pine-paneled bedroom had built-in recessed bookshelves, a desk, and bed. Toys on display are period-appropriate but not original to the house.

Through the deep-reveal doorway can be
seen the library's floor-to-ceiling tree
surrounded by beautifully wrapped gifts.
Santa stars in tree ornaments and displays.

STORYBOOK CHRISTMAS
The Kell House

For more than thirty years, the Kell House has celebrated Christmas by becoming "Santa House." To transform the house, a talented decorating committee begins the first week in November and continues over a two-to-three-week period. The goal is to keep the décor fresh and exciting. One year the stockings were new; another year, committee chairwoman Linda Patrick contributed a Nativity scene with oversized figures that graced the entry hall mantel. Returning guests are always eager to see what's new.

Holiday traditions are important at Kell House. While there are many events for children, two recurring key events for adults are the Candlelight Dinner and a one-night-only Candlelight Tour for friends of the museum. The tour takes place on the Saturday before Christmas. The electric lights are dimmed, and a guide leads visitors through rooms lit by tree lights and electric candles that re-create a sense of Christmas Past.

On display. There is much to see on a tour. The Kell family occupied this hundred-plus-year-old house until 1980, when they sold it to the Wichita County Heritage Society. However, it is still filled with original family furnishings. Some are connected with a particular family custom. For example, a red quilt covers a bed in one of the five bedrooms. When a daughter became engaged to marry, she would stay in this room until her wedding day.

The house contains extensive collections of textiles, art, decorative accessories, china, photographs, paper documents, and period costumes. Volunteers are trained to care for the fine woods, paintings, and silver.

House history. Frank Kell moved his family to a house on Scott Street before buying land on the bluff overlooking Wichita Falls. He hired the local architectural firm Jones and Orlopp to design the house, which combines colonial revival and neoclassical elements. Verandas are a striking feature of the symmetrical façade.

Kell hired a female contractor—his sister-in-law, Minnie Mae Adickes, to build the house. She began her career in 1906 as a widow with five daughters, the youngest only three months old. Construction began in 1908 and was completed in 1910. Adickes, who died in 1937 at fifty-seven years of age, built more than three hundred homes, with only a handshake for a contract. None are more impressive than this 5,500-square-foot house, with its still-working elevator, seven fireplaces, sunroom, library (with pool table), modern kitchen, and spiral staircase. Here Frank and Lula Kell reared their six daughters and son Joseph Archibald Kell, who died in a 1939 automobile accident. In 1911, a daughter, Sadie, wed Orville Bullington in the house. Family members lived here until Willie May Kell, their only unmarried daughter, died in 1980.

The Wichita County Heritage Society opened the museum in 1981. In 2011, the society began a capital campaign to fund a three-phase, $1.5 million renovation project to stabilize the structure, repair the exterior, and improve the interior. Work began in 2012. Through its education program, guided tours, and events, it continues to tell the story of those who founded and built Wichita Falls.

— WICHITA FALLS, TEXAS —

The Kell House balcony, decorated with seasonal greenery, welcome's Christmas holiday visitors. *Photography courtesy of Kell House Museum, sketch by architect David Strahan*

Below
A trio of arched openings executed in rich mahogany feature a gracefully curved grand staircase and the floor-to-ceiling Christmas tree.

A rococo-style marble mantel is the focal point of the formal parlor. Usually closed, the formal parlor was fully decorated and opened on Christmas Day to surprise and delight the Kell children.

Below
The banquet-sized dining-table set for Christmas dinner is surrounded by chairs based on an English William IV balloon-back design. The portrait over the mantel in the dining room is of Lula Kemp Kell.

Decorations on the bedroom mantel spell out Season's Greetings. A Christmas tree and vintage children's toys add joy. The tufted oval-back *bergère* is rococo revival, the era's most popular furniture style.